HOLIDAYMAKERS FROM HELL

Other books by Patrick Blackden

Danger Down Under
Tourist Trap

HOLIDAYMAKERS FROM HELL

Shocking Behaviour By Tourists Abroad

by

Patrick Blackden

First published in 2004 by

Virgin Books
Thames Wharf Studios
Rainville Road
London W6 9HA

ISBN 0 7535-0-863-X

Typesetting by Phoenix Photosetting, Chatham, Kent
Printed and bound in Great Britain by Bookmarque Ltd

CONTENTS

PREFACE

The stories in this book were gathered using various techniques, and it wasn't possible to source all entries. Also, I promised contributors that I wouldn't mention their full names, so thanks to everyone who sent me their tales – I won't embarrass you here; you've probably done that perfectly well yourself! While some of the stories are undeniably grotesque, they are presented in the spirit of humour, or to throw the spotlight on just how awful people can be. Not all holiday-makers are well-adjusted, civilised or pleasant individuals. The fact that I have included stories which, to anyone's mind, are pretty gross, does not mean that I condone the behaviour described, but it has certainly opened my eyes to just how far people (the Brits, especially) will go when they're off the leash. The worst excesses are here in fabulous Technicolor. If you are of a sensitive disposition and easily offended then you are probably best off putting this book down right now and buying a guide to wild flowers instead. You have been warned – herein are contained anecdotes of the worst holiday behaviour ever! It's the book equivalent of after-the-pub viewing . . . and on one of those disreputable cable channels that you wouldn't find your parents watching. I would beg readers not only not to try most of these activities at home, but also to try not to give them a go on holiday either. Hopefully you will learn something about holiday dos and don'ts in the following chapters, even on a brief flick-through. Before you think of joining in and adding to the statistics, take my advice at least on these three points: do try to make it to the toilet, always check for an Adam's apple and don't feed the lions. Happy holidays!

1. THE BRITS ARE COMING

'He who makes a beast of himself loses the pain of being a man.'

Dr Johnson

'If you want a shag, never puke on your bird's shoes. They don't like that.'

Russell from Stevenage, on holiday in Magaluf

The British abroad have had a reputation to live down to since the days of the Grand Tour, when privileged young men of the seventeenth and eighteenth centuries would drink and swive their way around Continental Europe, drunkenly abusing locals in fits of xenophobic fury. Among the more notorious English tourists of the time was the group that urinated on the Senate of Lucca from a balcony, and the young blade who, caught short in an Italian church, 'curled one out' on one of the pews. But as these gentlemen tended to travel with large bags of gold, their excesses were often either excused or used as pretexts for various scams and rip-offs in brothels, and at gaming tables, from Paris to Venice.

Sadly, foreign travel soon ceased to be the preserve of the rich or civilised. In the postwar years, increasing numbers of British tourists planned to forsake Bognor and Blackpool for sunnier climes, and by the 1970s their prospective Continental hosts thought it might be better if they were hemmed in to designated areas befitting their bestial behaviour. A string of reservation-style resorts sprang up, designed to contain holidaymakers insistent on drinking as much as humanly possible. Hence, the advent of architecturally brutalist zones such as those in Playa de las Americas, Tenerife and Magaluf, Mallorca – designed to ensure good drainage and to allow the vomit and blood to be sluiced off pavements and balconies with minimal effort. As long as the tourists were kept in one place, the idea seemed to be, they wouldn't ruin other resorts and they couldn't do too much damage. They'd also bring in a healthy income to those prepared to work with them. Yet over the past thirty years the drinking has increased, the behaviour has become more bestial, and more and more holidaymakers have found themselves spending balmy nights in the local slammer.

Behaviour at these resorts isn't actually so far different from what you'd see in any mid-sized British town on any Friday or Saturday night: public urination, vomiting and sex, fights, often involving bottles, loud singing punctuated by obscene rants, and inappropriately bared flesh. And the men are even worse. Such behaviour, whatever 'characteristic' English reserve some revellers may have had being long since eroded by a steady diet of trash TV and suicidal binge drinking, reaches its home apogee in British resorts such as Newquay and Blackpool. Here the infamous 'Ibiza lobster' comes home to roost, and gangs of young men and women alternately baring their sunburned chests or dressed in lime-green afro wigs and football shirts, get pissed, howl and throw up.

But there is something about actually being abroad that brings out the barbarian in the Brit. Maybe it's the heat, pounding down on those shaven craniums, frying brains unused to the liberty found in other cultures. The booze is cheaper, with a litre of vodka in Spain coming in at well under ten pounds, or a bottle of drinkable Scotch in Thailand just four; their partners, families and bosses are nowhere to be seen, and the weather does not – as in Britain – discourage public nudity. Some of the bars in resorts such as Faliraki and Tenerife also have a more enlightened attitude towards getting hammered: where in Britain would you be given a bucket to be sick into along with your drink, as is standard practice at Faliraki's Q Club?

There's no need to do without the great British amenities – toilets with seats included – either, nor any need to get to grips with one of those tricky foreign languages. Holidaymakers can now enjoy a mini-Britain with better sun, eating classic British cuisine including chips and gravy, chips and curry and chips and squid, read the *Sun* or the *Mirror*, and watch Premier League football in sports pubs and bars with names like 'The Dog's Bollocks' or 'Fuck U2'. A survey of British 18-to-30-year-olds who had visited Malia, Kavos and Faliraki during 2002, published in the *Daily Mirror*, found the following:

- 50% of the women drank until they suffered memory loss. The average alcohol consumption of all respondents was the equivalent of 22 glasses of wine a day. 52% had sex without using a condom; 16% had sex with a local, and 14% with a travel rep.
- Over the course of a two-week holiday, the men had sex with on average ten women. 64% flirted with women they weren't interested in; 60% said they had no intention of contacting the women they'd had sex with.
- Across both sexes, the average number of snogs per night was three. One in three respondents in a relationship intended to cheat, and of these 61% succeeded. Over a quarter of those surveyed had sex with more than one person in 24 hours.

In the 1980s, the Spanish Costa resorts boasted the highest number of Brits abroad – sun-worshippers keen to mingle with criminally inclined friends who had taken advantage of Britain's contemporary lack of an extradition treaty with Spain to stay in a villa with a swimming pool rather than be detained at Her Majesty's Pleasure. These resorts, which cover a vast swathe of the Mediterranean coast, provided the template for many that followed: vast, kitschy parodies of seaside resorts, apparently receding into infinite space, broken up by casinos, dodgy real-estate agents, and softly lit shopping arcades offering cut-price perfumes, swords and knuckledusters. Those bored of retail opportunities or settling scores with old lags can play a couple of rounds of golf on the Costa's surfeit of landscaped landfill sites.

It is estimated that over 300,000 foreigners live on the Costa del Sol, of whom the majority are British. Many retired Britons have come to live here, bemoaning the parlous state into which they believe the motherland has fallen, and keen to place a distance between themselves and the troubles back home, ranging from back-door taxation to imagined hordes of dusky asylum seekers steaming up Carshalton High Street.

Whether due to the high proportion of retirees or not, the Spanish resorts – from Benidorm to Torremolinos – now have a reputation for being, as one correspondent put it, 'places for middle-aged people to get drunk and party'. As most of the stories in this volume involve younger people getting drunk and partying, only a few of the Brits abroad stories come from the Spanish resorts. The more popular contemporary resorts for younger Brits abroad, and consequently the sites of some of the worst behaviour – and the worst stories – are often slightly further afield. In the following section they'll each receive a short introduction.

Magaluf, Mallorca

Otherwise known as 'Shagaluf' or 'Magalust', the popularity of this resort as a bargain-basement package holiday destination suffered in 1996 when local authorities won a court order allowing them to demolish twenty downmarket hotels. This was done in a bid to stop, or at least slow down, the characteristic 'violence, drunkenness and open-air sex' binges that took place every summer, and dissuade British holidaymakers in favour of the better-behaved and affluent Germans, who can be seen elsewhere on the island.

For some visitors in its heyday, Magaluf lived up to its nickname: a mid-1990s survey of 18-to-30-year-old visitors found that the average time between arrival at the resort and first sexual contact was 3 hours and 42 minutes. Why so long? For more recent visitors, however, such speedy work would be possible only for the least discerning, as men are now said to outnumber women by around five to one at the resort.

Playa de las Americas, Tenerife

Living in Tenerife, you tend to see your fair share of tourist misbehaviour. In the mid- to late 1990s, when the more commercial end of the British clubbing scene was at its peak and holidays abroad to continue this pastime were *de rigueur*, the notorious Veronicas area of Playa de las Americas was home to thousands of Brits out to have a good time by munting themselves with alcohol and a cocktail of other mind-altering substances. The results were often far from desirable. Some bad behaviour was the inevitable result of groups of lads just having more than their fair share of noted cat-piss substitute San Miguel. Tipping over bins, destroying signs, going to the conveniently placed Burger King over the road and deciding that the gherkins in their snack were better placed on the windscreens of passing cars than in their stomachs – petty acts of rowdiness, really.

Other uncivilised antics were due to the combination of cheap booze with people on holiday wanting to indulge in one-night stands. If there is somewhere in Veronicas that hasn't at some stage or another been used for sex then I want to see it, but the more exotic locations include the rocky beach in front of the complex (terribly clichéd but a great idea at the time), on top of a speaker in the middle of a club, and inside an enormous rubbish bin at the end of the street. By far the most obvious of couples that I have seen, however, was a man and woman who decided that leaving their stool at the bar in Tramp's wasn't strictly necessary since she was wearing a skirt and, of course, no underwear, and he could simply unbutton his trousers. Once the bartender had brought the couple to the bouncer's attention – he then asked them to leave – they nonchalantly stood up, smiled, and went into the toilets to finish off.

If all this seems pretty harmless so far, the uglier side to tourist misbehaviour is undoubtedly the fighting. Minor skirmishes outside the pub are nothing new, but tourists seem oblivious to the fact that picking a fight with the PRs that work the street is a bad idea, since they all know each other and can have a large amount of backup in a hurry. Perhaps the worst fight seen in Veronicas happened one St Patrick's Day, when the entire strip descended, no doubt with the help of some of the less discerning residents, into a mass fight between the Scottish and the Irish. Neutral holidaymakers with the taste for a ruck picked a side and joined in, and after several hours of chairs, bottles and people being thrown about all over the place the local Guardia Civil decided that enough was enough and went in with plastic bullets to calm everyone down.

Thankfully, depending on who you talk to, tourism of this type has been largely discouraged by the Canarian authorities, who have chosen to build more golf courses, shut down a lot of the Veronicas area, and encourage more 'five-star' tourism to the island. While this has left the dingier hotels without custom for the summer, and has put a few club reps out of business, the South of Tenerife is now a friendlier place for it. I just hope the residents of Corfu, Ibiza and Ayia Napa aren't too disgruntled at having a few thousand extra yobs to deal with. (CW, Bristol)

Contemporary visitors to Tenerife are probably more likely to have aggressive timeshare reps to deal with than to end up in a brawl or a three-in-a-bed romp. Still, if visitors are bored they can always visit the Torture Museum at the end of Playa de las Americas, a typical mainstay at Continental resorts popular with the Brits, whose ancestral thirst for public hangings is only whetted by such sights as the oral, anal or vaginal pear, an object somewhat like a sadistic Terry's Chocolate Orange, which would be inserted into the designated orifice then widened with a ratchet.

That's not to say that Playa de las Americas is now an altogether peaceful place. In July 2003 22 British tourists, 12 of them minors, were arrested for disorderly behaviour, following accusations that they had run riot at their hotel.

They were alleged to have thrown objects – including the contents of dustbins – into their hotel swimming pool, and to have damaged hotel property, including a table tennis table.

San Antonio, Ibiza

Ibiza has long had a reputation as a party island. Legend has it that the Roman army had a tradition of rewarding brave soldiers by sending them to the island for a fortnight with a galleyful of women and wine. Britain has no such arrangement with its squaddies, but has nonetheless been sending hordes of louts, yobs and party animals to the island for years. Many have been attracted by the island's reputation as the 'dance music capital of Europe', as well as by cheap flights and package deals to San Antonio, Ibiza's second town. While Ibiza used to have a reputation as an exclusive party island, by the time of ITV's *Ibiza Uncovered* documentary, which showed two girls who claimed to have slept with over forty men in a fortnight, the island had become synonymous with pissed-up Brits and casual sex. The behaviour of some of the British package tourists led the vice-chief consul, Michael Berkitt, to resign in 1998, stating that he hoped to 'never have to see another British tourist again'.

Much of the extreme British loutishness has been blamed on Ibiza's permissive atmosphere. David Daffalepa, manager of San Antonio's Amnesia nightclub, has pointed out that 'in England, life is more restricted. The rules of behaviour in Ibiza are so relaxed and they are not used to it. But the crazy thing is, we see them all doing that bad stuff and then they go out and stand in a polite queue for taxis, which Spanish people never do!'

Tourism in Ibiza is huge business, with the island attracting almost half a million British tourists a year, along with an estimated 200,000 Ecstasy tablets smuggled in from Liverpool and Manchester over the summer season. The authorities clearly don't want to stop tourists coming, but they have recently been making a concerted effort to ensure that only the right kind of tourists land on their shores. Strict guidelines have been drawn up with British tour operators, outlining the kind of behaviour that is deemed acceptable on the island, and tourism chiefs have been giving Ibiza an image makeover in an effort to draw more upmarket family-oriented tourists. Week-long package deals to the island used to cost around £200 – they now cost around £800.

Faliraki, Rhodes

The mantle of 'most infamous Brits abroad package holiday destination' has now moved from San Antonio to Faliraki, Rhodes. Once a fishing village, the resort was developed in the 1980s to attract family holidaymakers. In the late 1990s British tour operators began to build more budget accommodation and promote the resort as a new Ayia Napa, which resulted in a massive boom in the number of young visitors. Of the 430,000 British tourists visiting Rhodes annually, a third stay in Faliraki, but it wasn't until 2003, with the screening of ITV's series *Club Reps* and reports of numerous arrests of British nationals, that the resort was painted as some kind of modern-day Gomorrah in the eyes of the British public. Naturally, in the wake of all the fuss, bookings went up substantially.

Club Reps, a series which followed hopeful young Club 18-30-style reps through their training and showed the seamier side of life at the resort, was chiefly infamous for its exposure of the sexual exploits of two bisexual women, Rachael and Vanessa, who were seen variously indulging in threesomes and auditioning for jobs as pole- and lap dancers. The programme also showed loud American tourists looking for drunk girls to mount, demonstrating at least that the resort does not cater exclusively to Brits.

The ITV series was shown on Thursday evenings, and each Friday there would be an instant upsurge in bookings for Club 18-30 holidays to the resort, as well as a corresponding boom in applications to become a rep for the company. But if many males were lured in by the promise of cheap booze and easy sex, females – perhaps wisely – chose to stay away, leaving an uneven mix of five men to every woman. There were also reports of extensive drink-spiking, and of serial rapists descending on the resort, eager for some of the female flesh they'd seen on TV.

Operators of family holidays to the resort were horrified to see their bookings plummet, and while Club 18-30 did well from the 'Maz effect' (so named after the grouchy chief rep featured on the ITV programme), many of the other operators saw their profits fall. Package holidays to Faliraki cost around £200 for a week, leaving less margin for profit than is possible with costlier family-oriented packages. Local authorities blamed a perceived increase in bad behaviour on the programme's malign influence, and started to crack down on tourist yobbery, arresting thirteen Britons in one week. Among the incidents sparking these and other arrests were the following:

- An Irish tourist climbed up a flagpole outside a hotel, ripped the Greek flag off and ran naked through the streets tearing it to shreds.
- In two separate incidents British tourists were arrested for 'mooning' in public, both while welcoming a new coach load of tourists to the resort.
- Seventeen-year-old Patrick Doran was stabbed to death with a broken beer bottle in a bar brawl. Another British tourist charged with his murder admitted that he was culpable but told police that he had been so drunk he could barely remember why it had happened: police theories ranged from it being over a girl's flirting with two separate groups of men, to involving a spilt drink. Such behaviour is not uncommon in Britain: at a nightclub in Dudley, West Midlands in 1995 a woman's finger was bitten off by another woman who accused her of 'dancing in her area'.
- Another British tourist was killed when he was run over by a lorry. Rumours circulated that he had gone under the lorry as part of a bet with friends.
- Jemma Anne Gunning, an eighteen-year-old nightclub PR

girl, was arrested after stripping off in a bar when she won what has variously been reported as a 'Miss Bottom 2003' or 'Eurovision Thong' contest. She later admitted to having been 'drunk out of her head', and told press that before the arrest she had felt 'like the sexiest thing on two legs'. She said that 'I was just caught up in the moment. I was wearing two stickers over my nipples and people were all shouting: "More, more, more". I was dancing in the way I'd seen lap dancers dance on the telly – very sexually. I poured water over my head and then took the stickers off and danced for about another ten seconds.'

She faced an eight-month jail sentence after a judge told her she had insulted Greek values, but was released after paying a fine of over £1,500.

- Five holiday reps – from Club 18-30, Olympic Holidays and First Choice – were arrested and charged with conducting 'guided, illegal trade' during bar crawls, in return for commissions from bar owners. They were later released due to insufficient evidence.

Tour operators were blamed by local police for encouraging binge drinking with organised pub crawls, some offering a free pub-crawl coupon (ten free drinks) to any tourists who stripped off all their clothes. A meeting between Greek officials, representatives from the British Embassy and tour operators resulted in a ban on the pub crawls and on street drinking. Faliraki Mayor Yiannis Iatrides pointed out that locals were fed up with the behaviour of their British guests:

'Locals are not just upset, they're a bit frightened. By about midnight a lot of these youths are so drunk they begin undressing and running around totally naked. We Greeks would never do this in their country. It's quite obscene.'

A British police superintendent, Andy Rhodes, also travelled to the resort to advise local police on how to handle binge drinking. Rhodes headed Blackpool's Nightsafe initiative, a project restricting drinks promotions in an attempt to limit alcohol-related excess in Britain's premier tacky seaside resort. In a press statement he pointed out what few would have missed:

People go to Faliraki with the express purpose of getting drunk. It is purely a British phenomenon; not many countries in Europe have the same problems with binge drinking. What is happening in Faliraki is not any different from what is happening every weekend night in most towns and cities in the UK. What we are doing is exporting our problem abroad. It makes sense for us to go out there and show the Greek police how to deal with that problem.

Prague, Czech Republic
The advent of cheap flights to a wide variety of destinations means that British misbehaviour is no longer restricted to package holiday resorts. A number of European cities have played reluctant host to large groups of boozy Brits on stag dos and weekend binges, with Prague among the most popular. Many Prague bar owners are sick of seeing the

groups, usually identifiable not only because of their loudness but also their clothes: stag and hen do groups tend to wear drag or fancy dress, with one group of 53 women from Wales famously dressed as Tom Jones for a bar crawl. Some groups are barred from entry to certain pubs and bars, although other venues welcome the extra revenue they bring.

Despite the sentiments of one Prague police officer, who said that 'the Brits are more pleasant drunk than the Germans are when they are sober', the official police line is that the Brits are trouble. Jiri Sellner, Prague city centre's police chief, pointed out that 'They don't fight among themselves as they fight with bar staff, mostly because they think the bill is too high. They get angry and destroy something. Italians are wild, Dutch are wild, but Britons are the worst.' The Czech authorities are now in contact with Whitehall in an attempt to stem the rising level of crime committed by British men in the city.

Most British tour operators offering trips to or around Prague portray the city as somewhere punters can get cheap beer and cheap sex. One, 'Prague Piss-Up', is run by two Britons and offers stag nights, brewery tours and shooting lessons, along with trips to strip shows and bar crawls: 'You will spend about five hours travelling around the old town, taking in the sights and getting pissed.' Considering that one-way flights can be bought for as little as £11.50, British revellers have realised that it can work out cheaper – including accommodation – to fly to Prague and drink than to stay at home and drink.

Club Reps

Club reps – whose job is in principle to ensure holidaymakers have a good time, and in practice to get them as drunk as possible before signing them up for exorbitant package deals – came in for a drubbing themselves in the summer of 2003. Not only were several arrested in Faliraki for leading illegal pub crawls, but five others were also arrested in Kavos in Corfu. In the latter incident, the Greek media reported that two female reps performed oral sex on two male reps on a crowded public beach, and were later joined by a third rep and another man from the crowd. A local businessman captured the incident on video, which he later showed to the police. A censored version was shown on TV throughout Greece, both scandalising the predominantly conservative community and reassuring many young Greek men that English girls were indeed easy prey. The reps were reported to have resigned from their positions with Club 18-30, and the company apologised for their 'unacceptable behaviour'. But the incident probably did little to harm the brand in the UK, where its popularity centres around the promise of getting drunk and getting laid.

Club 18-30 was founded in 1965 to take advantage of the fact that young people in the swinging 60s had disposable income for the first time. Its massive boom in the 1990s – the company grew from taking 20,000 passengers at the beginning of the decade to over 100,000 by the end – can be attributed partly to cheap airfares and partly to the strong British pound: the average selling price of a holiday with the company is under £300. It now outsells any other competitor in the youth market by two to one.

Club 18-30's advertising has always courted controversy. In 1995 the Advertising Standards Authority (ASA) banned their 'Beaver Espana' poster campaign, which featured slogans such as 'Something deep inside her said she'd come again' and 'Wake up at the crack of Dawn . . . or Lisa or Julie or Karen'. Another poster, featuring the slogan 'Girls, can we interest you in a package holiday?' alongside an image of a man's crotch clad in boxer shorts, was also banned after a number of complaints, although it was still run in magazines.

A cinema advert in 2002 involving a mongrel dog watching Club 18-30 punters in bed then trotting off to have sex in a variety of 'human' positions with poodles, sheepdogs and Afghan hounds was slammed by animal charities, some of which dubbed it 'dog porn'. The editor of *Dogs Today* magazine was bemused: 'What sort of people would be attracted by an advert like this I can only wonder at. Dogs are dogs, but sadly there is clearly no restraint by those on 18-30 holidays.' The advertising agency responsible for the campaign, Saatchi & Saatchi, was at pains to point out that the dogs were not harmed while filming the ad, and nor did they actually have sex: instead 'strategically placed pet food' was used to help put the animals into position.

The company's latest online advertisement features three naked young men and one bikini-clad young woman on a beach. The men's rears are facing the camera, and the young woman, facing the men, has a hand raised in the victory sign.

17

Club 18-30 have also run a series of stunt marketing campaigns, including one mock demonstration outside the American Embassy in London, with people holding Club 18-30 placards and chanting 'We want Bush'.

While ITV's *Club Reps* was the first programme to have full access to Club 18-30 for the 2001 Faliraki summer season, others have followed suit. Also from ITV is *18-30 Stoners*, a reality TV show in which twelve people weighing between eighteen and thirty stone are sent on a Club 18-30 holiday. The overweight holidaymakers were allowed to spend their first week in seclusion at a villa where they could lose their inhibitions, before joining other holidaymakers and enduring their stares and comments. ITV billed the programme as an opportunity for a disadvantaged group to take part in activities otherwise unavailable to them, thereby restoring their self-esteem; but media agency Zenith took a more jaundiced view in their quarterly *Trends on TV* report: 'A simpler explanation is that we might as well make fun of fatties while it's still legal.'

Confession of a Club Rep

One thing people forget about repping is that it's really hard work. Out of the people that make it through the training, a few always drop out every season – they're probably just after one good night's sleep, but if they ask to come back they can't. Reps have a saying – I'd choose sleep over sex – because sleep's so much harder to come by.

You're not really meant to sleep with the guests, but most

people do. You've got to be careful about it, though. If you're a girl and you spend too much time with the boys, or a boy and you spend too much time with the girls, the reps call it 'chickening', and sometimes walk around clucking to let you know they've noticed. It's not a good thing to be caught doing, for all kinds of reasons.

But you're meant to be pretty liberal about other people having sex – that's half the point of why they're out there. A lot of the drinking games we play are designed to get people together. There's one, 'Battle of the Sexes', where we split the boys and girls up, get them hammered then put them back together, chanting to try and gee them up.

Some of them take it a bit too far, though. You get people having sex by the swimming pool, which some of the hotel staff get a bit upset by. It can be a problem when people slip over on the used rubbers as well, so we try and discourage that. Some of them just use the walls of the hotel to pee against also, which is just disgusting, and we've thrown people out if we catch them doing that kind of thing a few times.

The weirdest thing I've ever had to deal with was when two girls I was repping for told me they'd heard someone in their room as they were coming back from lunch. They didn't go in but went straight down to find me. I was a bit scared – you never know what you might find – but I found another rep and we went to check it out. As soon as we opened the door there was a commotion inside then something landed really heavily on the floor. It turned out that one of the other guests had got into the girls' room through the balcony – a lot of people leave their balcony door open, even though we advise them not to – and was using their knickers to have a wank! As soon as we opened the door he'd tried to get out, but his trousers were down around his ankles and he'd tripped up. So he was lying there half-stunned with this girl's lacy knickers round his dick, which was sick but also one of the funniest things I've seen on the job. We didn't want to cause too much of a fuss so we didn't get the police involved, but we did evict the guest. I think the girls kept their balcony door closed after that.

Sometimes the drinking gets a bit rowdy – a few of the games are pretty rank, like drinking through sweaty socks – but I'd never say it got out of hand, and it's just young people having a laugh, isn't it? We're not meant to drink while we're on duty, so we can always step in and help out if things go wrong. I saw one guy spray a can of shaving foam into his mouth, and if I'd been pissed I might have egged him on with the others, but as it was I helped him get it out without swallowing it – not too much of it, anyway. I did hear one story from the reps a couple of years back, which was that after one night out one of the guests pulled a manhole cover off the street and threw it through a kebab shop window. Then he stepped back and fell into the hole, breaking his ankle. I'm not sure how true that one is, though ... (AN, London)

2. FISHBOWL FIASCOS

What better way to immerse yourself in an alien culture than to sample the local brew? While this may on paper seem to be a laudable cross-cultural aim, in practice the notorious decision-fuddling effects of strange alcohol can land the adventurous holidaymaker in hot water. Predictably, some of the stories in Budget Bunk-Ups – the bad sex chapter of this book – also involve heroic alcohol consumption, but the following stories are for those hapless drunks who failed to get lucky . . .

Gran Tourismo

Coming back from nearly a month in Thailand we flew on Balkan Air – by far the cheapest choice of airline for the route, and not without good reason. The staff were rude, aggressive and focused solely on maintaining their rigidly sullen and unhelpful demeanour. The most common response to a query, whether it was to ask for a glass of water or to find out whether they knew when we'd be landing, was 'Noh'.

On arrival at Sofia, our second stopover on the flying equivalent of the milk train, we were offloaded into a largely empty airport that distinguished itself in two ways: one was that it stank of piss – everywhere; the other was that the entire upper floor was empty apart from a boarded-up bar and 4 non-matching pieces of garden furniture. Downstairs cats and dogs fought unchallenged on the concourse, and groups of tired, hungry tourists sat in small clumps on the cold marble floor waiting to get out of what looked alarmingly like photographs of the Warsaw ghetto.

Compounding these issues, the money we had changed on the way out was now virtually worthless due to hyperinflation, and nowhere accepted credit cards. Our answer to this was to pool our resources, and despite it only being just after 9 a.m., buy as much grain alcohol and cheap white wine as we could with the funds available. The result was that within 10 minutes all 15 of us were merrily tucking into plastic cups of fluid that both looked and tasted unnervingly like petrol.

From nowhere a stereo appeared, and before eleven in the morning there was a full-blown dance party going on in the airport, much to the consternation of its hatchet-faced staff. By 1 p.m., when our flight had originally been scheduled to leave, people were already extremely drunk, and it was then that someone managed to locate a supply of chemical stimulants, which did the rounds like wildfire. This wasn't just a party; it was turning into a rave.

Naturally the authorities had made multiple attempts to shut us down, from sending pilots over to shout at us to threats to call the police. None of us took them seriously, mostly because we were so messed-up that nothing really seemed to matter anymore, and the more glowering looks and hostility we got, the happier everyone seemed – if proof were needed that life in the West was simply about dancing and having a good time, we were presumably the most irritating evidence imaginable.

The flight had been delayed because of fog at Heathrow, which the rusting pile of bolts and aviation fuel we'd arrived on was apparently ill-equipped to deal with. The result was that nobody knew when the plane would leave, and we were all stuck in Sofia airport with no money, coming down badly from an entire day's worth of hard drinking and worse. If everybody hadn't been so tanned it would have been a heart-breaking sight. By now we were thirsty, hungry and unable to purchase anything to remedy either condition. The evening wore on and soon our planeload were the last sorry airport exiles still cluttering the dingy departures area. Nobody was really talking much, everyone concentrating on their own headache, stomach ache and shitty luck at being stuck in what we now suspected was going to be our home for the night.

My own evening was progressing particularly poorly: never having had an especially strong stomach and having been exposed to some virulent bacteria en route, I was starting to feel more than slightly queasy. I had headache pills with me, which went some way towards alleviating the searing white-wine hangover that threatened to burst my temples, but that did nothing to help my increasing sickness, and there was only one hope in my mind. In my hold luggage was an untouched 500ml bottle of Pepto Bismol, saved for exactly this kind of adversity because of its sweet stomach-calming anti-nausea qualities. If I could get to it, all my problems would resolve themselves, but without it, I was almost certainly heading for a head-to-head with Armitage Shanks.

By this point it was after 11 p.m. and, sapped of all hope, we slumped semiconscious on the sharp-edged plastic seating trying vainly to find a position that wasn't actually painful. It was at this juncture that one of the remaining surly officials yelled that we were to be put up in a 'travel hotel' and would have to reclaim our baggage before getting into the Balkan Air minibus. The relief when I clutched the cloth handles of my suitcase was palpable and, ignoring the hordes of fellow travellers busily tearing their way towards where their bags had been dumped on the floor, I set about digging for the sweet relief.

Within seconds I had the bottle in my hand, and instantly had its calming pinkness drifting down my throat – it would only be a matter of minutes now before all was well. Packing it back into my case, the world seemed a less brutal place: the airport seemed to be a few more degrees above freezing, the staff seemed only to be scowling rather than grimacing, and the contents of my belly, previously intent on hurling themselves from my mouth, suddenly seemed perfectly at home where they were. At that moment, the transport minibus arrived to take us to the hotel, was instantly mobbed by weary holidaymakers who moved more quickly than we did, and disappeared into the icy night. Even that did nothing to dampen my spirits, and we all stood about waiting for another car to arrive.

Meanwhile friends were making their way tentatively towards the exit in preparation and, in a tired fumble, someone walking past me let the bag they were carrying fall to the cold marble floor. The instant it connected, the litre of gin it contained exploded into glass shrapnel and a sea of alcoholic vapours. As soon as they reached my nose I realised the point of no return had been reached, and nanoseconds later a projectile rush of bright pink vomit issued forth, covering a surprisingly wide area of the airport's floor. My response was to try and get as far away from the gin as possible, so I began running towards the door and the cleansing cold night air beyond. But even the sobering blast of Sofia's frigid climate wasn't enough, and soon enough my liquid pink stomach contents were again communing with nature in an unpleasant and attention-attracting way.

Moments later two heavily armed police arrived, and it was with some disquiet that I noticed they had brought along their own non-matching guns – in my deeply fogged state, the fact that one had a pistol-grip pump-action shotgun and the other one an assault rifle seemed profoundly disturbing given that all police in England tend to be armed the same way – with a small truncheon.

No sooner had they arrived than they began softening me up. 'This is not a nightclub,' said one, stating something that I too had noticed. 'You cannot just vomit,' the other one added helpfully. I didn't really know what to say, so I just nodded and continued to breathe very slowly and deeply.

Unsatisfied by my response, and seemingly unaware that one of them should have been playing 'good' cop, they began demanding cigarettes – demands backed up by pretty unambiguous gestures with the barrels of their non-matching armoury. I was in no mood for this, and effectively told them to get lost, an attitude neither found especially agreeable. 'How you like we take your passport, you spend night in Bulgarian jail?' one asked. Even drunk and nauseated, everyone knows the answer to that question, and as I was about to hand them all two hundred cigarettes in my backpack the hotel bus tipped up, I ran at it, and twenty minutes later we were all safely sequestered in the paint-peeling austerity of an Eastern Block transport hotel.

We truly were ambassadors for our country. (NG, London)

A while ago, myself and two mates decided to drive around Europe. Seeing as our trip was mostly a quest to try new and exciting beers, what better place to stop at than the famed Haufbrauhaus in Munich, Germany. After setting up camp a couple of miles outside the city, me and my mates headed towards town. We bunked the metro and ended up at the Haufbrauhaus, where the oompah band is loud, the smallest beer you can buy is one litre, and the oversized waitresses carry ten beers at a time.

Several flagons later, I was chatting up this girl who was also staying in town, while my mates were singing with the oompah band. I was trying my best to convince this girl to leave the nunnery where she was staying and join us in our tent down by the river. She was showing some interest, but right about then my friends stumbled over and said they had to go. Since I figured I had a better than average chance with this girl, I told them I would find my own way home, and I'd see them in the morning. So my mates stumbled out into the night, at which point the serious drinking commenced.

A couple more oversized pints later, and it was time for me to go. I couldn't convince the girl to come back to my love tent, which was probably for the best since I was barely able to put one foot in front of the other. After dropping the girl back at the nunnery, I headed to the nearest metro station and hopped the first train. After a bit, I realised that I was heading the wrong way, and riding out of town. So I got off the train, and staggered around the terminal for a bit. I noticed these three German blokes giving me the eye for a while and then they started to walk towards me.

Well, I won't take that kind of shit. So in my beer-induced state, I drew my handy penknife, whipped it open and growled as I fell drunkenly to the ground. The Germans gave me a pitiful look, then wandered away. I picked myself up off the ground, wiped off the blood on my hands from where I had cut myself, then fell into the open doors of the next train.

Waking up a bit later, I picked myself off the seat that I had fallen into and wandered out the train doors into suburban Munich. I wandered around for a few hours and eventually made it back to my tent which, to my surprise, was still empty. Being as strung out as I was, I fell down on my sleeping bag and proceeded to pass out again. I awoke to one of my mates kicking me in the side as he stumbled into the tent half an hour later. 'I lost Tim somewhere in the city,' he slurred, 'I'm going to bed now ...' at which point he promptly fell down and passed out too.

I awoke at the crack of dawn when Tim stumbled into the tent and also promptly fell on the ground, breathing heavily and complaining about riding away from the cops on his stolen bicycle. The next morning, I got the full story: somehow Tim and Jake got separated, Jake managed to get back home, but Tim reckoned it was better to ride around the city on a bicycle he found unattended. The police pulled him over later telling him that it was probably better to ride with his bicycle light on, and safer if he tried riding on the pavement rather then swerving all over the road. (BD, Camberley)

We were in Cannes for the 14th of July, which unbeknown to us was Bastille Day (the Frog national holiday) and everybody local was preparing for that evening's firework display and celebrations. We started by downing a half pint of tequila (even though Mike was tricked into thinking it was vodka somehow) and then many pints of lager were hastily consumed.

On the way down to the beach (a mile away) we stopped at every bar for at least one pint. By the time we got there we were in a fairly boisterous mood, and with the locals already giving us evil looks, we just played up to them. Then it hit us.

We should join in the celebrations and give Cannes another reason to hate the English. So down went the bottoms and out came our pale English arses.

We went round the harbour seafront of Cannes, drinking more cans with photos being taken from all angles. We felt like celebs but we hadn't a clue what was soon to happen. As the day became night, the shows started and more people arrived to see our buttocks. We could tell that more people were being annoyed at us but we just thought, 'Oh, they're French, they're like that anyway.'

A group of five or six lads then proceeded to grab us, and to the sheer delight of the massed crowd around us, went on to strip us bollock naked and steal our clothes. It wasn't long before the local gendarmes became aware of two English perverts trying to ruin the most important day in the French calendar. Before we knew what was happening (and remember we could hardly see from the drink) we were forced to the floor, handcuffed, covered up and frogmarched (excuse the pun) to the police van.

The head copper could see us trying to talk to each other. After much shouting and swearing he proceeded to crack us both in the mush (fuck off must be a universal word!!). Nevertheless, I very much doubt anyone else has made page four of a local rag, with a report on how foreign scum should not be allowed into the country! (SE, Swindon)

One morning, after a massive sesh the night before, Dave decided to go and do a bungee jump. Obviously not a good idea, with his hangover, but we gave him moral support and came along to watch, stopping off for a full English on the way. He was looking pretty chipper as they put him in his harness, and we'd started drinking again by the time he was ready on the crane – best way to get rid of a hangover! Then he jumped off, and we cheered as he came down, only his face had gone all red, and right after the bungee rope had started to pull him up again he puked, spraying it all over the landing mat and splashing a few of the people watching. We couldn't stop laughing, it was the high point of the holiday, especially seeing him being lowered with drool still hanging off his mouth. The bungee workers were not happy with him at all. (MJ, Birmingham)

We'd gone to Alicante for a week, on a mission to get as pissed as possible and hopefully get laid. Well, I don't think anyone got laid in the end, mainly because we were too busy getting pissed, but some other funny stuff did happen. I remember we were walking back to our hotel from being out at the bars, and Steve's in the middle of the street stark bollock naked from the waist down. None of the rest of us had seen him taking his clothes off, and it wasn't like he was streaking either, just walking along calmly. This had us in fits, but we eventually managed to ask him why he didn't have his shorts on. He looked at us all anxious, like he'd been hoping we wouldn't realise he had his balls out, and told us he'd lost them. Then Barry asked him, 'What's that in your hand, then, big man?' Fuck knows why he'd taken his shorts off in the first place, but he was carrying them along in his hand and must have forgotten that he had them.

One thing I will say for us is that we didn't get in any rucks, however pissed up we got. But one night a Finnish bloke, pissed out of his tiny skull, as the Finns often are, kept on trying it on with us. He was a small fucker, so I don't know how he thought he could take us on. Anyway, he followed us about for a bit, talking bollocks, and we just ignored him until we saw some big green wheelie bins – the really big ones with the lockable doors. I looked at the others, and they knew exactly what I meant. We picked up the Finnish bloke, opened the bin and bunged him in, then pushed the bin down the street.

We weren't really thinking about what would happen if he hit a car, but he didn't anyway, thank God. Still, the sight of the bin spinning round down the street with his muffled shouting from inside was fucking hilarious. Then Barry starts chanting: 'Make way! Finn in a bin, Finn in a bin', as we were almost pissing ourselves, tears rolling down our faces. Then the bloke managed to get out the bin and stumbled around a bit then fell over. We couldn't believe it when he came back towards us, still swaying and still trying to start! So we put him in *another* wheelie bin and pushed him down the street again, bellowing variations of words that rhymed with 'Finn' and 'Bin'.

Our last night in Alicante was also Paul's birthday, so we decided to go out in style. He'd drunk half a bottle of tequila before we even went out, and after a few rugby songs and drinking games we decided to get him a slapper for his birthday. There was none of that going on where we were, so we went to a stripper bar. I think the bouncer wasn't too happy about letting us in, all off our heads, but we paid him a bit extra and we could go in OK. It didn't last for long. Paul stripped off down to his boxer shorts and got up onto the stage. The strippers moved away from him and the bouncers moved in, just as he was getting over-friendly with a pole. That was us booted out, and we had to dress Paul when the bouncer threw his clothes out the club – he was so pissed he couldn't stand.

When we got back to the hotel, we decided we couldn't let Paul's birthday end without him getting some action, so we decided to 'teabag' him. We got it all on film as well, and can use the piccies whenever Paul gets out of hand! Steve did the teabagging, squatting over Paul's face with his balls out and dipping one big hairy bollock then the other into Paul's open mouth. He snorted a bit when the first one went in, then actually started snoring with the second one in. Steve managed to hold still for a couple of pictures before collapsing in hysterics. I think Paul was probably a bit confused as to why he had someone's pubes in his mouth in the morning, but with a hangover like that it was the least of his worries. (AJ, Coventry)

Tenerife's calmed down a bit now, by all accounts, but a few years ago Playa de las Americas and Magaluf were kicking. We were there in the mid-90s, and when we rolled into

Magaluf early in the morning, having got a stupidly early holiday flight, people were already drinking. We checked in, got ourselves a lovely full English breakfast, then crashed out till the evening. We woke up to some loud music and the sounds of people laughing and yelling. We peeked out and all the rooms were full of people drinking and having fun. Everyone's doors were open and people were going in and out of any room they fancied. Some bloke stumbled into our room with a bottle of tequila and we started our night by necking some shots with him.

Later we went to the strip bars and clubs down by the beach. That's where we ran into Andrew, who was completely wasted and being wound up by some other blokes. Suddenly they started laying into him, while his friends just watched and didn't help him. So we went to try and help but they pushed us out of the way. I think some local lads saw what was going on – boys fighting girls – and they all came over to start fighting on our side. The boys got scared and got in their car. The local lads then ran after them and hurled rocks and bottles at their car. A few moments later the shiny black car had huge dents and scratches. Andrew told his friends to fuck off and he stayed with us for the rest of the night. We returned to our room and carried on drinking.

The next morning a hotel employee woke us up and told us we were getting kicked out. Andrew invited us to stay with him and so we moved to his room. During the day we went out and rented a car to explore the island a bit, and that night we went to a bar called Locos. The bar was a huge meat market and people were hooking up left and right. Since there was free beer, we guzzled as much as we could. So much that I agreed to ride a mechanical bull. So we made our way to this bar/restaurant/club that had a bull, paid our coins and got on. I only lasted about four seconds before I landed with my face buried in the mat. We then stumbled to another bar. That night was a blur but I remember our hotel room turned into a strip club. Before the night was over, we had blokes and girls dancing on the table, the girls naked.

The following afternoon we drove out to a beach a little way away from the resort area. Around three in the afternoon we ran out of beer so we decided to get more. We had unknowingly parked our car in a really sandy part of the beach and we got it stuck. We got some guys to help us but we couldn't get it unstuck. Eventually we found some locals with a tractor to pull us out, which cost us about £20. It seemed like they were working with an extreme sense of urgency, we didn't know why but we also didn't care. We soon found out, about fifteen minutes later, when the tide came in and the spot where our car had been stuck was under a foot of water!

On our final night there we went all out and got so plastered at Locos that the bartender refused to serve us any more. So we went driving around and we got pulled over by the police. We couldn't understand them, but it wasn't difficult to know that they were really angry. They started to arrest our driver and my other friend started crying. This got the attention of some guys walking down the street, and we asked them to come over hoping one of them knew Spanish. But they didn't and, by that time, our friend was sitting in the back seat of the police car! So we concocted a plan to try and rescue her. I jumped on the hood of the police car and started screaming 'la policia!' I got their attention and then one of the guys tried to open the car door but it wouldn't open. The police noticed and starting going at them. I got scared so I ran up to one of the cops and slapped him in the face and hit the other guy with a rock! They then started running after me, and while they were chasing me, two of the guys busted out the back window and pulled her out.

By that time they had me and I started screaming. The guys then came over and somehow one of them managed to get a hold of a handcuff and they handcuffed the cops together! We finally managed to scramble into the car and we took off as fast as we could. We made it back to the hotel, crashed and got out of town as fast as we could the next day. To this day I still can't believe that all this happened. When we tell this story, some people don't believe us, so then all we have to do is pull out the other handcuff with the Spanish engraving! (PL, Leeds)

I was inter-railing around Europe on my summer holidays in my late teens, and had ended up at some student party at Ghent in Belgium, drinking endless glasses of vodka and being told jokes by Lithuanian exchange students that had obviously lost something in translation. A band had been on, and when they finished they left some of their kit on stage, so me and another guy got up and started jamming on the keyboards, just messing around. There wasn't any other music in that room, so nobody seemed to mind, and it was fun – we must have played for at least a couple of hours, with people bringing us more vodka when our glasses were empty.

At around seven in the morning we stopped playing, and the guy I'd been jamming with started to get really maudlin. 'You know, man, you're lucky,' he told me. 'You have music in your blood. Me – I have nothing.' I tried to laugh off his suggestion, telling him that we'd just been jamming, it had been a laugh, just a bit of fun, and that was as much as anything what music was about. But my answer clearly wasn't hitting the spot, as he started crying, and telling me, 'You're killing my mother and father!'

As if this wasn't enough, he then attacked me, but really limply, trying to throttle me half-heartedly, repeating 'You're killing my mother and father' over and over again. It was weird – like he wanted me to hit him, or something, which I really wasn't up for at all. I pushed him off me and tried to get away. I spotted another guy I'd met earlier, a Belgian with a broken leg – it occurred to me later that he'd told me earlier he'd broken it while out on vodka, which I should have taken as some kind of warning – and decided to hang out with him and avoid the crazy man attacking me.

We went to the bar but found it closed, so just reached behind it and took a bottle of vodka each, and we made a decision to leave and find somewhere to dance. That's where my memory gives out, although I do remember it being around nine and standing in the middle of a crowded street, surrounded by commuters, necking vodka. Next thing I know, I'm standing in a room, singing loudly, beating and kicking on the door. It dawns on me slowly that my hands are badly bruised, and that my feet hurt as well – in fact, I'm not wearing any shoes. I sit down and stop singing. It is at this point that I realise my two front teeth are missing. Another revelation dawns – this is a cell, and I appear to have been put here for being drunk and disorderly.

The police were OK about everything, actually. They even tried to give me back the rest of my bottle of vodka, which I wasn't too keen on by this point, so I told the officer to keep it – he looked chuffed. But they did keep me in for a while, as I didn't have any ID with me and had apparently answered all requests to identify myself with the name 'Mickey Mouse'. They'd taken me to hospital as well, which I had no memory of, and apparently I'd been 'uncooperative' with hospital staff. Figures . . . (JL, Bristol)

We'd rented a house on the Costa, a bit away from the resorts and pretty rural, but we had a car so we could get around easily. One night we stayed in and just got hammered. Del was going at it particularly hard, and soon started to look a bit green. We were in the kitchen, trying to find something else to drink, when Del turned to me and said that I'd better find him something to puke in, or he was going to blow chunks all over the floor.

But I just couldn't find anything until I went outside and

got a foul-smelling pig bucket, from outside near the neighbour's farm. I turned to Del, who started to cover his mouth, and quickly handed him the bucket. He leaned over it and, after catching a whiff of whatever vile shit was in there, became violently ill. The next morning, not knowing what to do with the mess, I simply threw it over for the pigs next door, and to my disgust they were all over it like it was a Sunday roast! (JR, London)

My two best girlfriends and I were on holiday in Jamaica. The place we were staying at had an incredible all-inclusive package and drinks were free all day long. So, of course, the second we arrived, we were in the pool at the swim-up bar. I was so overwhelmed by the free drink deal that I decided to down over a dozen drinks of various different spirits in about four hours. According to my friends (I have no memory whatsoever after about drink number 7), my little party was just beginning. After taking a group shower, I decided to dart out of the shower and run to the balcony stark naked, giving the cabana boys a nice show. I guess all the running and booty shaking must have rumbled my tummy, because I then proceeded to throw up off the seventh floor balcony (starkers may I remind you, with the locals watching). And I managed to hit every single balcony beneath me. The locals were shouting at us: 'Oh my God' and 'Slackness' and 'Roughness' and screaming with laughter. This all happened at five o'clock in the afternoon! Luckily, I learned from that first day and, from that point on, I managed to pace myself a little better.

But I didn't shake my booty with such confidence after that. Shame. (HS, Los Angeles)

The Caribbean coast of Colombia has some of the world's most beautiful beaches, but most of the towns are resorts frequented by Western tourists, and I wanted to see what the purely Colombian villages were like. One German traveller I met recommended that I go to a small fishing village, the name of which I've inadvertently blanked from my memory. I stayed for about ten days. It was just as he'd described it: some Colombian tourists would come down at the weekend, but otherwise the place was pretty empty. I met a couple of characters selling jewellery on the street, and they helped me to buy weed; after a couple of days I was smoking crack with the chief of police over a poker game.

But I undid all the good work I'd done in getting to know the locals this way one evening, when I'd been out drinking. I didn't remember much of what had happened the night before, but I woke up at dawn, lying on the pavement by the sea. I was wearing only shorts – no T-shirt, no shoes, no glasses, no room key, definitely no wallet. My first thought was that I'd been mugged. I staggered over to the hotel I was staying in, and told them. The owner hadn't turned up yet, and I was invited to sit in a chair outside the hotel and wait until he arrived; then I'd be able to get into my room.

I sat in the chair and passed out. When I came to, a couple of hours later, I realised that I'd puked all over my front. Everyone in this tiny village would have seen me, walking on their way to work. Apologising to all and sundry, I fell into a shower and washed myself. Over the next few days strangers would approach me and hand me various items – my mangled glasses, my flip-flops – and tell me they'd found them on the rocks by the sea. Bit by bit my memory came back to me: I hadn't been mugged at all. I'd tried – feebly, if I remembered it right – to hit someone, and had fallen on to the rocks by the sea. I dimly remembered lying on the rocks laughing, as my companions for the evening debated what to do with me. At least they didn't kill me ... (IK, London)

One summer my friends and I decided to go abroad for an alcohol-fuelled holiday to Magaluf in Mallorca. Anyway, one night after consuming one too many beers on a bar crawl organised by the reps I decided it was time to head back to the hotel as I was becoming increasingly ill. I found the nearest taxi and jumped in absolutely hammered and asked the friendly Spanish man to take me home. Everything from that point is, to this day, still a blur and also an embarrassment.

It wasn't until the next day, when I awoke in my hotel room, that one of my mates informed me of what went on the night before. Apparently I had just got to the hotel in my pissed-up state completely out of breath as if I had been running from something or someone when one of my other friends, who was just leaving to hit the town, was greeted by the taxi driver who was not far behind, raging with anger. I had just thrown up in the front of his taxi and attempted to do a runner to avoid paying any penalty, let alone the taxi fare for bringing me back from town, failing to realise that in the state I was in it would have been impossible to escape a granny in a wheelchair let alone some angry Spaniard who was on a mission in a attempt to stop me. In the end my mate made me pay him the taxi fare and the measly £8 penalty that the Spanish driver had enforced on me the night before. (BE, Southport)

We'd started off our Ibiza evening as we meant to go on, going round a few of the bars having all kinds of stupidly named cocktails, probably so-named because they made you stupid. When it was time to go to Space, we'd had to balance out the booze with some other treats, which we indulged in while we were in the club as well. It was rammed and fucking mental, as ever, and I don't remember much else about being there except that I was loving it. Don't know when we left, or how we got back, but in the morning I woke up in our apartment lying on the floor, naked except for a T-shirt. And the T-shirt wasn't on my top, but around my middle – not wrapped around my middle, but with my waist through the neck. It was incredibly tight, and God knows how I managed to get it on; it took me an age to get it off. Before I took it off, though, I had to find the rest of my clothes. I searched all over the apartment, turning the place upside down, until I finally found them: folded and piled on top of my shoes neatly inside the cupboard where all the cleaning gear was.

And that wasn't even the weirdest thing. When a couple of the others had got up and we were starting to think about coffee and breakfast, we found that all the electrical equipment in the kitchen – fridge, kettle, you name it – had been unplugged. Not only that, but there was also half a courgette on the floor, looking mighty suspicious. None of us could work out what all that was about, although their looks prompted some guilty paranoia, I can tell you! Apparently I'd tried to get into bed with one of the couples I was with, and had been wandering around naked off my face. Probably a good thing no one could remember what had happened ... especially the part that involved the courgette. (JM, London)

On a recent trip to the Continent for a few England games, me and a mate decided to pop down to Luxembourg after our side's typical disgraceful performance. Driving into town, we thought we'd done all right – no shortage of totty walking around. Anyway, that night was the Grand Duke of Luxembourg's birthday (we didn't know who he was and nor did we really give a shit), and a local barmaid informed us that it would be like New Year's Eve all over again. This kind of lit the touch paper and we proceeded to make our way through every lager in the place and finished on these things that constituted half a pint of spirits. When we'd ventured into the bar the streets had been dead, but five hours later we left and the place was jammed. We made our way up to the main square and danced around to a funky band. The problem was that we were the *only* people dancing – two pissed-up Brits amid thousands of boring Luxembourgians – but this only fuelled our drinking.

A few hours, and drinks, later there was a massive fireworks do and things began to blur. The next thing I knew me and my mate were on some raised object (about 6 feet off the floor) and were trying to get the Luxembourg crowd going by dancing around on this 'roof' and trying to get them up there with us. For some reason they were giving us looks of disgust and wouldn't join us. Next thing we know there's a film crew in our faces and we think they're just filming the English having a good time. Turns out we were dancing on some monument to the Duke, the crowd were utterly disgusted by our behaviour and we were plastered over Luxembourg TV ... and we didn't even pull! (BG, Stoke)

Each year it is customary for a group of our mates to make the long trek to Spain via the 24-hour ferry in order to drench ourselves in our foreign neighbour's culture. As you can imagine, life on the ocean wave is not all it's cracked up to be – and with Kronenbourg in constant supply for a whopping fourteen hours, the effects of the commonly known (yet mostly misunderstood) disease of 'Ferry-itus' can set in all too quickly – except, that is, if you decide to hide from them.

In a novel approach to traditional remedies for the disease – such as to stop drinking, pass out, or knock yourself out – our friend Wayne took it upon himself to crawl aimlessly under a chair in the bar. When asked what the fuck he was doing he muttered the following: 'Shhh, I'm hiding – I am a seal!'

Needless to say that he has endured years of ribbing ever

since this debacle, more so even than when he disappeared into a cabin with another man (who had remarkable similarities to a certain P Stringfellow) the year before! On both occasions he has vehemently denied knowing anything about his actions. (TW, Hove)

A group of three expats, one working for a gem company, a magazine editor, and an English teacher, had been drinking heavily all afternoon and ended up at Soi Cowboy in Bangkok. They were denied entry at Long Gun, the street's most popular go-go bar, for being too intoxicated – which means they must have been incredibly drunk indeed.

Annoyed at this, they stationed themselves at an outdoor bar directly across from Long Gun and started taunting the doormen. The initial insults were producing little effect, so they upped the ante. They began insulting the King. This degenerated into 'The King is a wanker!' chanted over and over again. [Any adverse comments made about the King are highly taboo in Thailand.] Everyone in the immediate area was getting upset at this and several people started shouting at them. The police arrived shortly after this began. The three guys (who were by far the most idiotic they have ever been) were hurling abuse at the police, who were actually quite civilised about it, merely asking them to fuck off home before serious trouble erupted. To reinforce the point that they were policemen and should be heeded, one of them partially drew his gun. The magazine editor (the ringleader, with a reputation for flamboyance that sometimes bordered on genius, though not on this occasion), fell to his knees in front of the police, spread his arms wide, threw his head back and said: 'Go on then, shoot me. Come on, what's the gun for? Shoot me!' Incredible.

The other two suddenly sobered up a bit, looked around them and realised that the situation was a bit out of hand. They convinced their friend to get back on his feet and leave. They headed up the road to return to their motorbikes – about a two hundred metre walk. My friend, who witnessed this, said he saw the police talking with the Long Gun bouncers, and then a posse of about fifteen guys was quickly arranged. Armed with sticks, they went after the three idiots. They timed it so that they caught up with them at the end of the street, just out of sight. They chased them down and laid a beating on them with boots and canes. Two of them ended up in hospital, but were discharged shortly after, with a few cracked ribs, cuts and bruises.

Obviously, the gang had been told to go relatively easy on them, or they like as not would have killed them. Considering what the lads said about the King, it's amazing they were able to restrain themselves. Shortly after this incident, one of the guys went into AA and hasn't had a drop since. (CW, Bangkok)

3. BUDGET BUNK-UPS

Holidays provide an opportunity for sexual adventure, away from the pressures of working life. Points systems, foam parties and excessive cocktails ensure that everyone gets a portion – as long as they don't look *too* closely. One tip for anyone worried about falling into the same trap as our first correspondent: look out for the Adam's apple. That, along with the large hairy hands dragging on the floor, tends to be a dead giveaway.

What I did in my Summer Holidays
I had finished my A levels and was on my middle-class gap year. I had saved a few hundred pounds for the trip that my friend and I had planned which was to be a tour of Southeast Asia. It was far away from all the boredom of Europe and cheap – two fundamental things we needed. John, my travelling partner and long-time friend, had sourced the cheapest way to get to Bali, where our three-month tour was to begin. Full of anticipation of the exotic we set off on our marathon flight. First we flew to Helsinki, then Bangkok, then Jakarta, and finally to Bali.

Bali was a bit of a disappointment when we landed there the first evening. The first thing that we saw in the resort of Kuta Beach was a 50-foot pole with the giant golden arches on top ... Don't get me started! But we did soon acclimatise to the humid evening air and found a cheap hotel.

Our first day was spent on the beach trying to surf as well as any young man brought up in London could. Trust me when I say that the waves are fucking big and drop you into a tumbling hell of white surf. We persevered and met a couple of other guys from the UK who knew where the best bars were, and so we made arrangements to meet up that very evening for large amounts of cheap booze consumption.

John and myself met our new-found friends in a bar on the main strip that was built like an old ship, in the vein of a miniature *Cutty Sark*. We started to drink a local concoction of loads of white spirits mixed with orange squash and served in a funfairesque goldfish bowl. Needless to say that the desired effect was soon happening when bowl three turned up. It was soon time to move on to the Sari Club, which was the best place to go. I do vaguely remember turning up at the gate to the club, where there was a security guard only letting in Westerners. All the hawkers selling watches, sweets and fags were kept out. Once in, it was a full-on banging, drinking, dancing frenzy – perfect. We continued drinking heavily and were probably really loud and obnoxious, but not as loud and obnoxious as the Australians, who would win hands down every time. The drinking continued and another move was planned to another club called Peanuts, which was very close apparently. So eventually we made a move to leave the Sari Club. Our group had grown to about seven or eight completely pissed people.

When we went out of the gate of the club we were greeted by a myriad of hawkers and others, including beautiful petite prostitutes who mingled into the scrum we had caused. One grabbed my arm and asked me where we were headed. I innocently said Peanuts, and she said she'd show me the way, promptly marching me down a dark alley on the far side of the road. As soon as we went into the shadows she whispered in my ear 'you wanna fuck me . . . you wanna blow job . . . you wanna fuck meee?' And to be honest I did. I was a long way from home, and it was something that seemed almost a rite of passage. That and five litres of booze in my tummy saying 'yeah la la la Booo BOOO llaa laa la' – in fact it seemed like the most natural thing to do.

I would like to point out two things at this point: I was nervous about what I was doing and it was dark. I mean, it was really dark. As soon as we were off the main drag it got pitch black. There was a hut/garage that my beautiful little lady was taking me towards. I couldn't see jack, but she made a beeline for it, found the door and flicked on the light. It was a small room with nothing in it apart from a single bed. We went in and she fell to her knees and pulled out my very large erect cock and began to suck me off. After about a minute she stood and said, 'You wanna fuck meee?' I reached into her pants, saying, 'Yes.' At this point I found a small erect penis in her/his pants. Now this was a shock. She/he continued unperturbed, 'You wanna fuck mee?'

Well, I was so confused all I could muster was 'How?' She/he led me to the bed and lay down. At this point I think I made a concise decision that I had come this far so I may as well. She slipped a condom on me and guided me into her/him. We did it face to face, which I wouldn't advise. All the booze was messing with my mind, but my knob was on a mission.

When I was done I stood up, unravelled a large roll of cash and threw a handful of bills on her/him, then turned on my heels and left. I went back to the main road and saw John calling my name and looking bemused/pissed. I said I'd got lost and headed for the hotel where I de-robed, washed about ten times and threw away my clothes.

It took me about three days to venture out at night after that, and we soon left Kuta and headed to the interior of the island, which was beautiful and awe-inspiring. The rest of our trip was, as you'd expect, an interesting drink and drug-fuelled tour of Southeast Asia.

Over the following years I let slip to a couple of friends what had happened, although John was and still is none the wiser. My name has been changed by my friends, who now always put 'queer' in front of it. I didn't think about it that much apart from the inevitable, 'Oh shit, I might have AIDS!' thoughts that plagued me until a routine blood test gave me the all-clear. (CO, London)

In Q Club in Faliraki one summer I was in the bathroom pissing at the trough right next to the exit door. I was at the end, nearest the door when, all of a sudden, this girl pokes her head around the corner, and sees me standing there with my dick in my hand. Anyway, as I am mid-piss, this girl looks directly at my package and says, 'Hey, nice dick.' What was even better was that it was a bit warm in the bathroom, so I was at showcase length. The only response I could muster was 'um, thanks' because I was so stunned. That said, I quickly snapped out of my bewilderment and proceeded to finish my business. I asked the girl to dance. Fast forward about three minutes . . .

My dick is now out of my trousers and in her hand. If you have never tried to dance on a packed dancefloor while being jerked off, you must try. It's not that easy. To cut a long story short, I think I offended every girl within ten feet of me. I repeatedly heard 'that's sick' or 'you pervert'. Maybe so, but I wouldn't have done it any other way. And hey, what about the girl doing the jerking?

Needless to say, I was unable to finish. It's very difficult to concentrate when a group of people are watching. Who knows what happened to the girl? We stopped and then went our separate ways. But, that's the beauty of 'Raki . . . there's always another girl. (JC, Chelmsford)

On Mark's stag do in Amsterdam, we ended up doing what most groups of men on a stag in Amsterdam do – visiting a brothel. It wasn't really a success: everyone had nosed up a bit, and the prostitutes were none too impressed by seeing our coke-shrivelled maggots. Worse still, none of us were able to come, either, and after having paid for fifteen minutes each, our first visitor (me) was unceremoniously kicked out and replaced by the second.

'Ach, you have the same problem, ja?' the prostitute asked, seeing another wizened dick. This friend managed to get it up eventually, only for his fifteen minutes to end before he did. Hoping that he'd found the legendary 'tart with a heart', he begged her to help him come, even if it ran over the short time. Reluctantly she agreed, lubed up her hand and started to toss him off at a furious pace. My friend later told me it reminded him of a self-lubricating steel mill, such was the force of her pumping.

All in all, the experience left us grotesquely humiliated, out of pocket and one of us with a horribly chafed old chap. (AJ, London)

A guy that I used to know named Mark and one of his friends, Paul, decided to go skiing for a winter break. They headed to a resort in the French Alps, Meribel, which is known for having a pretty young crowd. And as they'd expected, the place was packed full of holidaying students letting off steam.

One day, after a hard day on the slopes, Paul and Mark hit one of the numerous bars. After a few rounds, they spotted three girls talking to one guy. They moved in to pounce on the two available girls. After talking for a while, the six of them decided to head back to the girls' hotel room to get better acquainted.

When they reached the hotel room, Mark started kissing the girl he was with while Paul was getting lucky with one of the others. Things moved pretty fast for Mark, and he and his girl were soon both naked on one of the beds. She was straddling him and told him that she would like to tie him up. Mark thought it was pretty cool that she was so kinky, and agreed. Big mistake.

She instructed Mark to close his eyes as she bound both of his arms to the bedposts. Once she had secured the knots, he was completely helpless. When he opened his eyes, he had the shock of his life. The guy whom they had seen with the girls in the bar was now on top of him, naked. He was licking Mark's nipples and slowly making his way downwards. Mark (understandably) freaked out and began screaming for Paul to help him. Paul was submerged under the covers in one of the bedrooms with one of the other girls. He popped his head out to assess the situation. Despite Mark's pleas for help, Paul advised him to 'go with the flow, man. Go with the flow.'

Yet again, Mark yelled at the guy to get off him, and at Paul to help him out. Fortunately for Mark, the guy got off (not like that!) and Paul decided to leave his girl long enough to untie his old friend. And as soon as he was freed, both Mark and Paul got their clothes on and ran out. (ID, Ipswich)

The following story took place on the outdoor terrace of a bar right in the centre of Laganas, Zante. The terrace is long and thin and right on the main drag. A couple who had been getting pretty frisky in the bar came outside to the terrace. The guy sat down in a chair and the girl came and sat on his lap. They were getting very horny and seemingly unaware of all the people around them who by this point were starting to watch what was going on. The girl hitched up her skirt and they started fucking in the chair, her straddling him, completely oblivious to the fact that there were by now lots of people standing around watching. The whole encounter finished abruptly when she pissed all over him, got up and walked off, just like that! She didn't even say anything to him, just got up, wobbling slightly, pulled the back of her short skirt back down, and left this bloke sitting in a chair with his knob out, covered in pee, surrounded by onlookers. (TW, London)

For our mate Lee's stag party we went to Ibiza for a long weekend. We'd been having a wicked time but realised towards the end of the weekend that we should really send him off in style, and formed a plan based on some of the sleazier things we'd seen in the bars in Ibiza Town. Basically a couple of us went off to try and recruit a tranny – some of them look just like girls, you'd never know the difference, especially if you weren't expecting it – to meet us at a foam party that night and give Lee a very special treat.

So we're all at the party that night; it's our last night, so we're making an extra effort to get as trashed as possible, then the boys who'd gone out on the mission earlier spot the tranny. This was the first time I'd seen her – or him, I should say! – and I have to say she looked stunning, especially for a bloke! So they give her the nod, pointing out Lee, and she starts to make her way over to him. They start dancing, and he looks round at us with the cheesiest grin, so we all grin back, thumbs up.

Then they start pumping the foam out, and everyone goes wild – the girls are pulling their tops off and flashing their tits, everyone's snogging, there's even a few people shagging by the speakers and in the corners. As for us we're just waiting for the time Lee puts his hands in the tranny's pants and goes fucking mental – we had to watch anyway as we didn't want him to get in trouble, especially as the tranny'd brought her own minder who was no doubt getting an eyeful as well. So they start snogging, and we give a cheer, then they move off to the back of the club. Well, it's going to look like a bit much if we all troop after them, so John goes down to have a look at what's going on.

When he comes back it's like he doesn't know whether to laugh or cry. We ask him what's going on, and he tells us the tranny's giving Lee a hand-job. Hilarious! Perfect – and what's Lee doing? He's only giving the tranny one back!

When he came back he was wiping something off his hand with a tissue, and looked a bit embarrassed. It wasn't what we'd expected, to be honest, and I don't think anyone let on that we knew. We just carried on getting more pissed. (SO, Croydon)

Four of us had gone on a walking holiday in the Lake District. We'd rented a cottage for a few days near Windermere, and Nick had brought his dog, as he didn't really want to leave him for someone else to look after. Everything was going according to plan – long walks with sandwiches to eat on the peaks, pub dinners then more drinking when we got back to the cottage. On the third evening we'd all been hitting it harder than before, and Nick had been laying into this bottle of tequila he'd brought specially for the trip. We'd all had some of it, slamming shots, but he'd just been swigging it from the bottle, and we reckoned he'd probably just pass out in a while. And I'll bet he wished he had.

He went off for a bit, and we probably thought he'd just gone for a piss, but then he called out to us to come and watch. So we pile out, only to see him with his trousers off, standing there in his socks with his dick in one hand and a tin of dog food in the other. 'What the fuck are you doing?' someone asked.

He giggled, smeared some of the dog food on his dick then said again, 'Watch this!' Then he called for his dog, which bounded over happily, tail wagging and ears bouncing, and started to lick the dog food off you know where. If we hadn't been so drunk we might have tried to stop him. As it was we just stared for a bit then left when the food was finished and the dog just kept on licking. I don't think any of us was ready for that, however much tequila we'd drunk.

It was kind of funny, in a sick way, but it put a damper on the rest of the holiday. I couldn't look at the dog without thinking about what it had done, and Bill got really freaked when it jumped up in his lap and started licking his face. As for Nick, I think most of us have lost touch with him now. (SW, Bournemouth)

On our first night in Faliraki we'd gone out to Bar Street and Club Street to kick off the holiday in style. We avoided all the ticket touts and got loads of free drinks off the lads in Sinners, where they'd give you a fishbowl of spirits if you danced on the bar with them! Lethal! After a couple of these they gave you a bucket as well to puke into if it got too much! Claire could hardly stand, and I wasn't much better, but that didn't stop us carrying on, and we ended up at Q Club, which was mental. They have these poles there you can dance around, and there were a few other girls showing off around them, with all the blokes standing around and clapping, so Claire decides she'll have a go. Trouble is, she hasn't got any knickers on! Obviously the boys go crazy, and loads of people are taking photos. Claire didn't care, and I thought it was hilarious, though I can't believe we made it back safely that night. She was so embarrassed about it next day though, and wouldn't go out to Bar Street for a few days. (NP, Reading)

Last summer a bunch of us went to Amsterdam with my uncle and some of his mates, all 50-year-old rockers. I don't know if it was that they didn't want to be shown up by the young upstarts, or they wanted to impress us, or they were just like this the whole time, but they were deeply embarrassing from the word go. Even on the plane one of them kept on making sordid suggestions to the stewardesses, asking one of them repeatedly if she had anything to suck on. It just got worse when we landed, with them going into a bar with no money, ordering loads of drinks then arguing over whose round it was before leaving without paying. Probably most of the bars were happy to see the back of them, even if they hadn't paid.

The most memorable incident involved one of them visiting a prostitute. He was called 'the Slug', I never really worked out why, and obviously they'd all gone window shopping in the red-light district and a couple of them had ended up with some tarts. But the Slug got kicked out when he'd gone too far with his one – when we asked him what he'd done he said 'I was only trying to kiss her tits', and it's true that you normally have to pay more for stuff like that, but knowing him I'm sure it was something much darker – and when he realised that he'd had some stuff nicked out of his trousers in the room, he stormed back in. She was with another bloke by now, but he pulled the two of them apart and demanded to get his stuff back. Somehow he managed to get everything he'd lost and escape without being stabbed to death. Lucky Slug. (PH, Bristol)

Faliraki 2002. Kranky vs a Geordie bird. One night, while we were all standing in a kebab shop, a girl turned to Kranky and said, 'Don't pinch my arse.' Kranky declared his innocence, and she turned back to him, screaming, 'Don't touch what you can't have!' and squirted a big bottle of ketchup over his shirt. Kranky later had this to say – 'Stupid slut, I didn't even pinch her arse.' (SB, Swansea)

We were in Ibiza for the first time on our summer holidays. The first night me and my mate met up with two sisters at our hotel. They asked us to take them to a nearby club, and they were pretty fit so of course we accepted the invitation.

At the club, me and my mate played 'scissors, paper, rock' for choice of the sisters. I won and chose the younger, riper one, then confidently led her out onto the dance floor. Immediately, I could tell that she was into me and soon we were having a snog. Then she pulled me off the dance floor because she didn't want her sister to see us. I asked her to leave, but she couldn't leave without her sister. Looking for a little privacy, we eventually found our way upstairs to an area of the club that was 'off limits' that night. We sat down in front of the bar and carried on kissing. All of a sudden, one of the bouncers showed up and was yelling at us. I told him how sorry we were and that we would leave. But, surprisingly, he motioned behind the bar and winked at me. So I took his cue and the two of us went behind the bar and started going at it again.

Now out of sight, I pulled her underwear out from under her dress and began sticking my fingers inside her. She in turn took out my dick and started giving me a hand job. Then, I pulled her on top of me getting ready for the plunge. Before we actually started, I happened to look behind me and was shocked to see that the same bouncer was there, watching –

with a huge smile on his face. He had been there the entire time, watching us! I quickly zipped up my trousers and picked up the girl and we got the fuck out. And I'm not absolutely sure, but I think he had his hand in his pants all the time . . . (CS, Cardiff)

A few years ago a bunch of old school friends got together with me and we went to Benidorm for a week of madness. There were plenty of good stories from the week but one by far takes the cake.

The first day we were down by the beach, we met a few fit birds and my mate Neil especially took a liking to one of them. So we went out with them drinking and having a laugh for the next couple of days and nights, but alas nothing was happening between Neil and the girl he was after.

When he realised that he'd probably never get off with her, his frustration started to mount. Instead of wanting to simply get a shag out of her, it degraded into wanting to 'hate fuck' her. And from that point on, we started to refer to her as the 'hate fuck' girl. To add to the fun Neil kept chanting it like a mantra.

We didn't see much of those girls for the few nights after that, which only added to the drama. Finally, it was our last night and we met up with them for a final party in their room. As the night progressed everyone got wrecked as usual. And at about three in the morning, we noticed Neil had disappeared. At about four, the rest of us finally headed back.

We got back to the room and much to our horror found

Neil passed out on the bathroom floor, knuckles bleeding and trousers and pants around his ankles. We woke him up and asked him what the fuck was going on. His explanation was priceless and one I'll never forget: 'You know I just wanted that girl so badly that I finally gave up and came back here, jerked off and then punched the sink.' (OP, Camberley)

Me and my girlfriend were in New York, and had been having a few drinks in a noodle bar. Suddenly I had an idea about how we could spice up our evening, having checked out the swank hotels nearby. I took her by the hand, walked her into the Hyatt and straight past the desk clerks, who didn't look twice as we walked into one of the service corridors. There I spotted a kitchen door, and looked through the window – there was nobody in there, and the door was open. No sooner had we got in there than I got her on the draining area of the sink, legs spread and knickers off, rubbing herself. One thing led to another, my lust overcame my adrenaline, and we had a shag in the kitchen.

When we'd finished, my girlfriend started to load up her bag with the silver cutlery lying around, which seemed like a really bad idea in case we were caught leaving. I managed to convince her to leave it there, which was probably just as well as I then saw a face at the window in the door – someone had been watching, God only knows for how long. We walked up the service stairs to the first floor then hopped in the main lift down to the exit, chatting with an elderly couple there about how good the kitchen service was! (JG, Birmingham)

When we were in Ibiza we met a girl going on a remarkable journey around the island's men. Using just one word she managed to pull again and again, including three of my friends. Her original chat-up line to Paul was '22?' The journey took a brief halt when Craig refused to become '25', using the 'I have a girlfriend' excuse and scarpering, but she carried on undaunted and managed to pull my mate Dave by the end of the evening.

We later found out that her and her friends had a points system for getting off with blokes – twenty points for getting laid, ten for giving a blow job, five for getting off with another girl and three for a bloke. I think the girl we met beat her friends hands down ... (PS, Southampton)

My mate Ron told me this one. In August 2001 a German tourist, described by police as a beautiful blonde, was arrested at an Israeli airport after being found naked and begging men for sex. She told police that she had been working as a kibbutz volunteer in northern Israel over the summer, and as she had a few hours to kill before her flight she'd decided to search out men for sex.

One man she encountered walking through the car park agreed to her suggestion, and they had sex between parked cars. She was then spotted, naked and waiting for another man to pass, by a routine police patrol. Police put her on a flight home and told her to behave better in future. Maybe she'll come my way one day at Terminal 3 in Gatwick. (KS, London)

61

A friend of mine was on holiday in Amsterdam with his girl-friend and some others, and bought an S&M-style outfit for his girlfriend in one of the red-light district shops. That night he popped some Viagra and, when his girlfriend had put on the outfit, he rather over-excitedly embraced her. The head of his cock was caught in one of the buckles and a chunk was torn out of it. It was extremely painful, but the Viagra was keeping him hard. His erection would subside, then he would see his girlfriend in the outfit, and his erection would spring up, spraying blood over the carpet.

His girlfriend gave up trying to help him and joined his mates in the next room, where they hurled abuse at him while he stood under a cold shower for a few hours trying to get his hard-on to go away. But the Viagra kept on kicking in again, and he eventually had to wind an entire roll of toilet paper round his cock and go to hospital with a massive bulge in his pants. (AW, Glasgow)

Me and my mate Alison were out on the piss in Ibiza Town when we decided to go for a wander around the back streets – don't ask me why. Anyway, we were both bra-less and up for fun, and we were hoping to pull later on in one of the clubs, but it was still early evening and there was plenty of time. I knew Alison was more pissed than I was when we passed by a couple of local lads standing around their scooters and they started calling out to us, 'tits out for the lads' and she obliged. Up went her skimpy top and out came her great Geordie jugs. The funny thing was, they weren't

English; they were locals. They'd obviously picked this expression up from the tourists. Next thing I know, things had gone wild and the two boys were all over us. I kept saying, 'you sure?' to Alison, but she was loving the attention. Actually, the boys were quite sweet and polite, really, and couldn't have been older than sixteen. Next thing I know, Alison tells me to wait while she takes the both of them over the road to this piece of scrubland. Fifteen minutes later I'm getting really bored when she comes running back triumphant saying: 'Two virgins in one day and it's not even nine o'clock.' She's a wild one, is our Alison. (LP, Sunderland)

4. TOILET TRAUMA

Delhi belly, Montezuma's revenge, unusual toilets, open sewers ... foreign holidays can strike terror into those with delicate digestive systems and be an endless source of amusement and fascination to the scatologically minded. Some of the following stories involve tourists who definitely need a crash course in toilet training!

Catastrophic Khazis

Nkatha Bay, Malawi. I could feel a stomach bug coming on – I was bloated, and already had the runs. At the time I thought that if I abused my body enough, anything living inside it would die, and decided to put this to the test by drinking a small bottle of whisky. Firmly believing that this was medicinal as well as fun, I found that the first bottle went down so well that I bought a second. Unfortunately halfway through this second bottle disaster struck. The toilet at the place I was staying was a tiny, unlit hole in the ground – and just that, dug out of the earth – in a wooden shack. It was night-time, and the fact that I was very drunk combined with the lack of light and urgency of my jet-hose evacuation meant that I somehow managed to smear the results all over myself: not only on my legs and arse, but over my upper body as well. I stumbled out, naked, having lost my underwear in the process, and my friend found me outside, stumbling around and telling him that I needed help. Barely able to stop laughing himself, he found a hose and hosed me down, for which I am eternally grateful; I think he even managed to field any awkward questions about the state of the toilet.

It could have been worse. We heard a story about a girl who'd actually fallen into one of these holes, and had spent the night down there. By the time she was rescued in the morning, she'd had a nervous breakdown. (JM, Bristol)

I ended up in a town about two hundred miles from Bombay that I knew was rarely frequented by Western travellers. You could tell that by the lack of street-side stalls selling the usual luxuries to soft travellers like me – namely toilet paper. So inevitably I developed serious runs and inevitably my supplies of toilet paper ran out. The only thing keeping me on the right side of acceptable hygiene, psychologically crucial to someone caught up in this predicament, was a rapidly thinning bar of soap.

In my hotel room the shower, a misfiring, spluttering contraption emitting jets of water in all directions but the one in which it was pointed at, was combined with the toilet. There was a hole in the ground that combined as an outlet for water from the shower and the splattering liquid from my rectum.

After a few squats over the hole and sluicing it down with

a jug of water I decided I needed a shower. As I was washing myself down with that one precious item – the razor-thin stub of Imperial Leather – the soap shot out of my hand. I watched, disbelievingly, as it hit the wall and rebounded at an acute angle. My disbelief turned to horror when it skidded towards the hole, eluding my desperate scrabbling hands. It even had the audacity to spin around the hole a couple of times before disappearing down it.

There was no choice in the matter and I didn't, indeed couldn't, give myself time to think about my next move. I plunged my arm straight down the hole and fished about in unknown and unthinkable depths. After some very long seconds I managed to extract the soap. I spent the next ten minutes ferociously scrubbing and washing my arm and I ate left-handed that night. (AC, Glasgow)

In 1995, I went on holiday to Spain with my girlfriend, her parents and younger sister. After many hours of travelling from my home in South Devon, towing a caravan, I was understandably knackered so I didn't get much drinking done that first evening. When I woke up the next day I decided that I was going to have a beer or two, so the first stop was the local supermarket for the ammunition for the battle against my liver. After paying only about £3.00 for a tray of 24 bottles I started drinking like a man on a mission.

After many bottles, a barbecue and the Spanish heat I started to feel queasy, so I decided that there was something wrong with the beer. The course of action was to switch to drinking some noxious local spirit with a good 45 per cent kick. By midnight we were all ready for bed so I stumbled as best I could, held up by my girlfriend and her mother, to the toilets wearing T-shirt and shorts. As I stood peeing I felt a good fart build up and let it rip. Unfortunately I followed through, which kind of sobered me up a little. I got my shorts off as quick as I could and checked for spillage, but thankfully there was none. By now my girlfriend and her mother were outside the cubicle telling me to hurry up, so I did the only thing I could and used the outside of my boxers to wipe my arse (there is hardly ever any toilet paper in Spanish campsite toilets). As soon as I was as good as I was going to get I tried to flush my £1.99 Marks & Spencer's pants away but alas, this was me and nothing ever goes quite to plan. They got stuck. So, it's gone midnight in the middle of Spain, I'm as pissed as a newt and I'm trying to force a pair of very unpleasant boxer shorts around the U-bend while my family is banging on the door and asking whether I'm OK or not.

I eventually got them far enough around the bend to leave and I slept naked that night with my girlfriend, who has never forgiven me. Unfortunately the following morning, as we went out for the day, this little lady was wandering out of *my* cubicle with a big pair of rubber gloves and a sodden pair of M&S boxers – held at arm's length. (BF, Torquay)

I was walking along taking in the sights and sounds of the local market in Jaisalmer in India when a somewhat unusual sight absorbed my attention. A peanut seller was squatting on a low ledge set in a wall over a large pile of his wares. Unknown to him, but in full view of all passers-by, his genitalia had slipped out of his lunghi and were delicately resting on top of his peanuts. I was just thinking to myself how his potential buyers, despite his appendage being so obviously visible at eye level, did not seem to be repelled – in fact they were queuing up ready to argue and bargain. Then the ground gave away beneath my feet.

My short downward flight into this hole in the street was mercifully interrupted when my feet squarely landed on something hard and I heard a distinct but heavy splash. A second later I became aware of a moist warmth seeping through my trouser legs as I stood at waist level to the street feeling bewildered and somewhat bemused.

A large number of laughing Indians surged forward to hoist me out of the manhole and back onto the street. The same number surged back when a rank and hideous smell emanating from my trousers overwhelmed the heavy market fragrance of spices, cooking and street food. I stood in the middle of a wide circle of market traders and passers-by who kept their distance as they examined my trousers. From my waist down to the top of my knees was cream material, but from then on the rest was brown, thick and gleaming with the slimy detritus of raw sewage sludge. Clumps of shit were falling from my trousers onto the ground with soft thuds. To add insult to injury the peanut seller, still wonderfully oblivious to his genitalia nestling in his peanuts, was holding his sides and doubled up with laughter.

There was a pause as I stood on the end of much pointing and arguing and many sympathetic but amused waggles of heads. I shrugged my shoulders and adopted a look of majestic dignity as if this whole incident was far too trivial for my attention. The crowd hurriedly parted as I made a slow, ponderous return to my hotel, trying to walk in a way that didn't allow my trousers to clutch at my legs, trying to ignore the terrible smell wafting up with every squelch of my shoes and trying to ignore the slime curling around my toes. (AC, Glasgow)

Ian and two of his mates were kipping in a car park in Biarritz on a surfing holiday, during which it rained for about two weeks solid. They were woken up one morning by an angry Frenchman and his wife and daughter shouting. It turned out that Ian had laid a huge turd on the welcome mat of the French family home. They were chased from their sleeping spot to shouts of 'Cherchez le police' and 'Le grande merde'. (MM, London)

I've worked at Disneyworld for the past few summers, and have seen some pretty base things happen. Last summer was one of the worst, when a Brazilian tourist dropped his trousers in the middle of *Honey, I Shrunk the Audience* and took a dump in the cinema. It had to then be closed for cleaning and sterilisation. (BN, Miami)

When we went to Tenerife last year, we all wanted to have a big week of shagging and drinking. And oh, didn't our dreams come true. We can't remember much of the holiday, except one occasion when my best friend Toni got really drunk and had alcohol poisoning – yeah, funny, but what she didn't realise was that she would have a bad case of the runs. When we went out she didn't want to be left home alone so she came too. We were all having a really good time, until Toni had a desperate urge to go to the toilet. She went to the toilets but they were all taken with people being sick, or they were closed. So she made a run for it to the gents. But she was too late and by the time she got to a cubicle she had a turd in her thong. We were all really pissed off 'cos we had to go home early so that she could have a shower and clean herself up. She's never drunk so much again. Still, we could have been even more cruel and given her a wedgie! (HW, Basildon)

We'd been in India for a few weeks and there was rarely a time when at least one of us wasn't ill. This time it was Charlie's turn, and he had giardia, some horrible amoebal infestation that had him bringing up huge eggy burps and sending him to the toilet every ten minutes. We'd arrived in Jaipur earlier in the day, and were staying in a really nice guesthouse, with perfectly tended flowerbeds, which were clearly the owner's pride and joy. But not for long. Charlie suddenly raced out of the room, not for the first time, and came back about five minutes later, looking exhausted and pale, and went to sleep.

After about an hour there was a knock on the door, and the owner poked his head round. 'Somebody in here is very ill,' he said, his tone half accusing and half sympathetic. It turned out that Charlie had found all of the toilet cubicles busy, and hadn't been able to hold back, so had sprayed his shit all over the owner's prize flowerbeds. We managed to placate him with a handful of rupees, and I think one of their staff must have washed the flowerbeds down with a hose, as next time we saw them they were clean. (AB, London)

I once heard a story of a man in a restaurant in Bangkok . . . As it was a small restaurant the door to the toilet led straight from the café area. He went to the loo and feeling a bit weary rested his head on the door while doing his business. Unfortunately he fell asleep. Even more unfortunately the door gave way and he fell headlong into the middle of the table area, crowded with diners, with his trousers round his ankles and a turd lodged halfway out of his arse. (SF, Bangor)

We had rented this cottage in Scotland and had managed to procure all kinds of narcotics, grass and alcohol. Inevitably the weekend turned into a complete binge and some time in the middle of Sunday afternoon we decided it would be a good idea to go for a walk and see some of the beautiful countryside that we had travelled up to enjoy but had yet to explore. We left Ed sitting on the sofa utterly drug-addled and quite happy to contemplate the scenery through the window.

When we returned a bit later Ed was still sitting on the sofa, but was also slumped forward – his head and arms uncontrollably flailing about as he tried to pull up his trousers from around his ankles. Our mounting concern at what on earth he had been doing turned to horrified amusement when we saw that he was sitting in the middle of a damp patch on the sofa.

We hauled him up to his feet and as he stood up there was the sound of two soft thuds from behind him. We looked around and two turds, moulded by the shape of the cleft of his arse and hardened by incubating body heat, had fallen onto the carpet. He stood swaying, trousers still around his ankles, genitalia hanging free and looking dazed and quizzical at our shouts and catcalls. Then, slightly misunderstanding us, he said: 'I went about an hour ago. I was in there for about twenty minutes', and pointed to the door of the toilet. We all simultaneously pointed down and when he looked down he was even more puzzled. 'What the hell are those? Who pulled my trousers down?'

And then it slowly dawned on him.

'Aw jeez. Oh no. No. No No.'

Once his shocked shouts and curses had subsided he then said: 'Listen. Can we keep this to ourselves? I mean we've all done this kind of thing, right? Don't tell the others.'

The problem was half of us had already disappeared, thumbs clicking on mobiles to do precisely that. (LC, Liverpool)

5. DIRTY TRICKS

Whoopee cushions and hand-buzzers don't really cut it for the contemporary generation of tourists, who have a slightly sharper sense of fun. With friends like these . . .

We'd had a right laugh in Faliraki, but the Essex birds next door to us were a bit too much up their own arses, complaining if we were playing music late and not really up for having a laugh. So we left two-week-old milk in the sun for two days then pissed in it and poured it in the four corners of their balcony on our last night. Trust me, it stank like fuck. (SB, Swansea)

On our first night in Ibiza one of the lads – we'll call him John – started drinking properly for the first time. Needless to say, he got shitfaced and started talking to some really ugly girls, then carried on until he was drunk beyond belief, so we ended up half carrying him back to the room.

When we got back it dawned on us to play a prank on him. We got an egg and took out the yolk, dropped the white of the egg down the crack of his arse, pulled his pants down a bit and took off his shirt. Then we got a girl from next door to put on some lipstick and kiss him all over, and borrowed some clothes from her and her friends.

John woke up the next morning with no memory of what had happened at all. When we told him he'd left with some bird that looked like a bloke, he lost it, and started getting really scared he'd taken it in the arse from a bloke in drag. For four years we didn't tell him it was us. (SC, Cornwall)

While in Malia in a drunken and sleepy state I had an unlit sparkler put in my mouth. I didn't really know what was going on until, on opening my eyes, I saw flashing lights and to my dismay realised that some evil git had lit the sparkler. But all the lads were stood around and piled all their bottles in my lap ready for the pic to be taken by Biccy across the way, so I kept it in, not wanting to be a killjoy. Unfortunately a large group of people thought it would be a great idea to stand in front of the photographer and generally admire the décor and craftsmanship of the really cool bar we were in. Here's the really unlucky bit . . . The sparks were now singeing my eyebrows so I had to spit the sparkler out, and it subsequently somehow hooked in my watch. I had a choice here. Tonight's beer or my arm? Well, I decided that if I didn't have an arm my beer holding capacity would be greatly reduced, so I threw all the bottles everywhere, which caused broken glass and beer to rain down on everyone while I ran around in a three-foot circle screaming like a pansy trying to get rid of the sparkler that was burning the flesh off my arm.

We left very shortly after on account of the fact that all the people there were going to show their appreciation to the guy who threw the bottles – Oops! Well, I now have a permanent sort of Africa-shaped scar on my arm. It was a cool night, though. (FC, Taunton)

Faliraki 2002. Earlier in the day, Iceman had bought a straw hat off a dodgy gypsy woman. Later on that night, Ice is chatting up a couple of girls on the table next to us, and asks if any of us have a light for them. Isaac walks over and hands him the lighter, then, as he's walking away, sets the back of the hat on fire. Within seconds, the hat has five-inch flames on it and Ice is so pissed that he doesn't realise. The girls scream, 'Get that hat off!' and Ice replies, 'But I like the hat! Don't mock the hat!' (SB, Swansea)

On our second night out in Faliraki, we all got pissed up and headed back to our hotel. Stu fell asleep dead drunk in my bed, which I was none too happy about, as I wanted to do the same thing. So we tried to wake him up, first by throwing water on his face, but that didn't work. So we thought we'd have some fun. First off we got some scissors and cut off chunks of his hair, and gave one of his eyebrows a trim. Then we got some warm water and put some shaving foam on the bits where we'd cut his hair and his eyebrow, and shaved them. He still didn't wake up, even though we were pissing ourselves doing it.

Some girls came back to the next-door room, and they must

have heard us laughing, 'cos they came in and wanted to join in. It was one of their ideas to tie him up by his hands and feet, then cut a hole in the back of his jeans and show off his hairy white arse for a few photos. Then we had the bright idea of drawing on his arse with a magic marker, a big arrow pointing to his arsehole with 'Cock' written next to it. Actually we went a bit mental with the magic marker after that, which was one of the things that upset Stu most as it was a bugger to get off. He wasn't too happy about the jeans or the shaving either – he had to go out next day to get all his hair shaved off so he looked like less of a nob – but the thing that really got him upset was after we got back, when we sent the photos to everyone we know and put them up on a website. He didn't talk to us for months. (SG, Cardiff)

While on holiday in a hotel on the Isle of Wight I became friendly with an elderly chambermaid who had a sense of humour, so I decided to play a practical joke on her. The guests of the hotel, myself included, were due to go on a coach tour for the day. I knew she would be cleaning my hotel room so my wife and myself set about making a dummy under the bedclothes; we used a pillow for the torso, towels shaped to look like legs, a pair of shoes sticking out of the bottom of the quilt and a wig placed on the pillow. I placed a fizzy-drink bottle under the quilt where it appeared to be a willy, but it didn't look quite real, so I began to mould it with my hands.

At this point my wife noticed the window cleaner appear at our window, much to our amazement. He then disappeared, somewhat embarrassed, having obviously assumed I was doing something of a sexual nature to what he thought was a man in the bed. We then left our room to board the bus for our outing, and as we were doing so I noticed the window cleaner going about his duties. I thought I would take it a bit further and winked at him – he was so embarrassed he almost fell off his ladder. (RT, Tyne & Wear)

Before setting off on holiday I dreamed up a practical joke to play on my sister-in-law and her partner, who I would be travelling with. I prepared the following petition, which was to be presented to them by the manager of the hotel we would be staying at:

Petition

'We the undersigned urge the hotel management to evict the guests of Room 29 for making excessive noises including loud moans and groans, and causing a general nuisance.'

This was followed by a series of made-up names and addresses, including those of a policeman and the local vicar, all of whom had hotel room numbers. I arranged for the manager to confront them at the bar in front of the other customers. The manager was very convincing. She refused to serve them a drink and told them they were to pack up and leave. They stood at the bar, mouths wide open in total disbelief, as the manager showed them the petition full of imaginary names. (RT, Tyne & Wear)

A trick I often play when holidaying in a caravan park is to throw any surplus bread on friends' caravan roofs. This is done in late evening, after the sun sets. As soon as day breaks, hopefully around four or five in the morning, seagulls and crows descend on the caravan roof to feed on the bread. The noise they make as they peck at the bread and hop around is deafening. This replaces an alarm clock and never fails. The trick should be played on the last day of your holiday, so that it cannot be played back on you. It is especially effective if your friends have had a good drink the previous evening and hopefully have a bad hangover. (RT, Tyne & Wear)

Tourist information staff in Newcastle were bewildered when a Dutch tourist walked into their office wearing a frilly pink shirt and carrying a Polaroid photo of his car in a car park: he wanted to know if they could tell him where his car was. It emerged that he had come over on the ferry from Holland with some friends, and while he had still been sleeping it off after a marathon drinking binge his friends had not only dyed his hair but also taken most of his clothes and hidden his car before catching a ferry back to Holland.

Happily the tourist information office staff were able to help the hapless Dutchman, by identifying the car park in which the car had been left. They gave the man some money for food then reunited him with his car; car park attendants decided to waive the charge which had been building up, leaving the Dutchman with fond memories of Geordie hospitality.

6. MINDLESS DRUG HOOVER

Many holidaymakers indulge in narcotic binges on holiday, not least because drugs are often cheaper and more readily available abroad than they are at home. But from red-eyed Brits clogging up Amsterdam's coffee bars to tripping Israelis clinging onto their sanity by their fingernails at Thai beach parties, it's not always such a good idea. While some of the people in the following stories were probably having a lot of fun, others would have been far better off tucked up in bed at home with a warm mug of Ovaltine.

Nuclear Chill

We'd enjoyed a few of the Big Chills in England and decided to go to one of their holidays abroad, on one of the Greek islands. I'd taken some drugs out with me, including a bottle of liquid acid, just the thing for finishing off a session. I shared it with a few other people when we were out there, and we'd had a really good day. At about five we could see that a storm was coming in, and decided to go back to our room to get ready for going out that evening. Most of us were in couples, and so we all had someone to go back with.

All except one of us, who was a guy, Nick, out there by himself.

We were changing in our room when we heard a knock on the door. I went to open it, and Nick was standing there, all wild-eyed and soaked from the rain. He looked confused, so I asked him what the matter was. He took me by the arms, looked me straight in the eyes and told me. 'They've done it! They pushed the button!'

I was still none the wiser about what he was on about, and asked him. He told me that there had been a nuclear strike – he'd seen the mushroom cloud on the horizon – and that probably only this island had been spared. My girlfriend was laughing by now, but I knew the guy was serious, and really worried. I tried to reassure him by looking at him as sincerely as he'd been looking at me, holding his shoulders and telling him that it wasn't true. 'Look, you took some acid, and there's been a storm. That's all it is, a storm.'

But you could see that he didn't believe me. He had the fixed, glazed stare of someone who thinks that only he has the answer – that the rest of the world is insane – and after shaking his head a few times, he wriggled free of my grip and ran out of the door into the rain. My girlfriend told me to leave him; he'd come down eventually. But I felt responsible for him, having given him the drugs in the first place, and went out into the storm to try and find him.

When I did, he seemed a lot calmer. He was in the bar by this point, drinking slowly. He still had a bit of a crazed glint in his eyes, but we probably all did. It was only when I overheard him muttering – 'They don't understand. It's all over' – that I realised the poor deluded fool was still convinced the world had ended. I thought for a while then came up with a plan to convince him. 'Nick, how about if I call up a friend in England and ask him if everything's OK? Will that be good?'

He stared at me, then nodded, perhaps keen to have his apocalyptic vision proved. I don't know what would have happened if my mobile hadn't worked. I was probably a bit anxious myself by this point; his madness had started to infect us all. I rang a friend of mine, Richie, back in London. Anxious faces surrounded me as the storm thundered and I broached the subject. 'Hi, Richie, how's it going? Any news to report from London?' I paused, barely able to believe I was going to ask it. 'Any – nuclear strike?'

It hadn't happened. Obvious, really. And fortunately this did calm Nick down. But it could have been any of us. (AH, London)

It was the summer of 1999, and a friend and I were going to Australia. We'd been living together for a few months, and getting into some pretty heavy cocaine abuse; we'd been up all night before the flight, and even on the way to the airport we'd had a line or little booster every fifteen minutes or so, or at least it felt like that! When we got to the airport we met up with my dad, who works for BA and had managed to get us upgraded to Club Class.

Once we'd gone through into the departures area we

continued our fifteen-minute treats, and liberated a Dunhill lighter and watch, worth about £200 each, from the duty-free shop. But it took a while for us to board the plane, and by the time we were in our comfy Club Class seats we were getting twitchy – our booster was long overdue. After a quick discussion we decided to have a line on our seat-front tables as the plane was taking off: the cabin crew would have taken to their seats, and we put a magazine in between our seats so the people behind us couldn't see anything.

I took out a big rock and crushed it on my table, then racked up two huge lines. I did the first one as the captain dropped the throttle, then my friend did his as the nose of the plane left the ground. We let out a huge whoop as the plane took off, high spirits that we managed to maintain throughout the flight by repeating as required. (TG, Brighton)

How Blue was my Valley

'You will come with us to the station. Now.' Call me intuitive, but I could tell the Kenyan policeman barking these orders was serious, even though I didn't care. Maybe it was his three colleagues surrounding me; maybe it was the shotguns they were toting; or perhaps it was the tank-like meat wagon parked alongside my budget guesthouse that gave it away. Deep down, beneath the haze, I knew I was in big trouble. But the part of my brain that had previously processed logic had ceased to function. I couldn't control the delirium dictating my actions; I was crazed.

'No, I'm not going anywhere with you,' I roared back at

him. 'Fucking make me!' I may have even shoved him. The cops stared at each other with a mixture of amused fascination and abject incredulity. How this skinny, malnourished tourist could be resisting four of Nairobi's tooled-up law enforcers in a dusky alleyway simply beggared belief.

Compounding the general vibe of confusion surrounding this unusual street scene, they actually backed off, still exchanging befuddled glances. 'You write your name and address,' proffered one of them, bizarrely. I complied with this request willingly enough, scribbling down phoney, expletive-ridden contact details on the scrap of paper he handed me.

If my distraught friend and travel companion James hadn't intervened, who knows what would have happened. As it was, he managed to persuade the cops that I would compensate the taxi driver for jumping all over his parked cab, while he watched me from the coffee shop window. And the next morning, after waking with a head that felt like lead soup, and with a burgeoning sense of dread washing over me, I paid the driver $35, which seemed cold comfort for the dents in the bonnet and roof of his livelihood I had made, but he accepted.

Believe me, I don't normally behave like this. Let's face it, if I did I'd probably be in jail or dead. So what had caused this unprecedented bout of suicidal taxi trashing and cop-baiting? Valium, that's what – and one beer.

Valium is popular among the backpacker set, who use it to knock hours off the dreary 15-hour-plus bus trips round Asia.

It's so simple: just neck a blue and wake up at your destination, having eliminated the usual transit nonsense – the vehicle breakdowns, lack of leg room, the malfunctioning aircon, surly non-English-speaking bus crew etc. Many Asian pharmacists are wise to travellers' recreational use-and-abuse of Valium, and have bumped up their prices accordingly, though you can still buy it over the counter. But, as with most things, just because you can doesn't mean you should.

My 'African Incident' was the result of a burgeoning taste for these pills developed over the course of two months spent backpacking round East Africa during summer vacation from university. It wasn't as if I'd just discovered Valium, either. As an undergraduate in Nottingham, I and fellow student wasters had used the little blue pills to ease the comedown effects of hectic bouts of clubbing. We'd all hustle back to someone's hovel at 7 a.m., saucer-eyed, sore-limbed and wired, to share the fruits reaped from a pharmacist friend who would regularly restock our chemical supplies.

But while Valium was a precious commodity on campus, in Tanzania it was easily available from local chemist shops; you could buy dozens for a quid or so and, intending to return to uni like some heroic, gift-bearing narcotic Dionysus, I stocked up. I'm not sure why I raided this stash so frequently; I think it started off as the aforementioned travel aid, but pretty soon I was popping them for the hell of it, then traipsing lopsidedly after my companions in a tranquilised stupor. I started to have blackouts, coming to in a new town in Uganda with no idea of how or when we'd arrived.

My friends were concerned but, unaware of the extent of my mounting habit, and aware of the fact that they weren't my babysitters, were content to shake their heads and prop me up when need be. I don't think I was ever close to getting hooked, although my tolerance level certainly increased. By the time I arrived back in Nairobi, a couple of days before my flight home, I needed to pop multiple Valiums just to feel it. The night the cops came, I'd had seven during the course of the day (if my memory serves me correctly, which it probably doesn't). We'd gone out for a beer, and after a few sips I was bouncing off the walls like a deranged rubber band. Level-headed James had quickly ushered me out of the bar and was trying to get me back to the guesthouse before I did any damage. That's when the unmanned cab lured me from the shadows with its trampoline-like façade.

It only occurred to me afterwards that people commit suicide by boozing on Valium. That's how far gone I was. (JQ, Thailand)

All Valled Up and Nowhere to Go

When I was in South America in the mid-1990s you could get both amphetamines and Valium over the counter fairly easily. I used to tell chemists that I felt carsick on long bus journeys, or was terrified by the huge drops by the Andean roadside, and one of these would normally work. What was tricky was getting the dosage right. Some of the speed pills were meant to be slow-release, so you'd have either to shave them with a knife or chew them up to get the full effect. This time I'd

85

done the latter, with a batch which turned out to be stronger than I'd anticipated, on a long bus journey from Arequipa to Cusco, in Peru. An hour into my journey I was having a great time, listening to my Walkman and grinding my teeth, but eventually I realised that I should probably try to come down. I'd bought a packet of Valium, or rather some Valium-like drug, for this purpose, and in my speed-crazed delirium decided to eat all of the pills in the packet. Well, it worked well enough. Eventually I was fast asleep, drugged into oblivion.

Next thing I knew, the bus driver was shaking me, trying to get me to wake up. We'd arrived. I knew I'd feel groggy, but this was terrible. He managed to get me to stand up, then my momentum helped me to stumble down the aisle and out of the door – and then the ground came up to meet me. Fast. I'd been chatting to a Colombian man earlier and had told him what I'd done, so he had some idea what kind of state I was in. The kind man helped me with my pack and to find some-where to stay. I didn't even remember getting there.

Eventually I woke up in a bed in a room. I was starving and disoriented. I hadn't eaten for around 24 hours, and knew that a meal would make me feel a lot better. So I went out, just wearing a T-shirt and a pair of shorts, no idea what time it was, to find something to eat. For security I left my pass-port and most of my money behind. But there was nowhere on my block, and by the time I'd turned a few corners I was lost. This didn't strike me at first – I was still looking for somewhere to eat, and it was only as I finished my meal that

I realised I might have some problem getting back. The problem wasn't helped by the fact that it was now dark outside.

Still, I raced out and half-jogged around the streets, hoping that some familiar landmark would jump out at me. Nothing did. It was then that the rain started. Huge, icy drops, straight off the Andes, had me soaked to the skin and chilled to the bone within seconds. I took refuge in a hotel lobby, and tried to explain my predicament to the receptionist. She was friendly enough, and wanted to help me, but I couldn't remember the name of the hotel, and I could see them losing interest as I pored over the phone book, hoping that one name would jog my memory. None did, and there was no way they were going to let me stay there for free.

I wandered out onto the street, seriously worried now, and was just about to go to a police station and throw myself on their mercy when I spotted my Colombian friend eating in a restaurant. He saw me too, and ushered me in. He took me back to his hotel, lent me a towel so that I could have a shower, and even arranged a spare mattress to be brought in so that I could sleep on the floor of the room he was sharing with a few friends. A true gent.

He gave me the address of the place the next day, and I went around. It was a monastery, and the door was locked with a padlock. I spent a while trying to get someone's attention, but there was nobody around. So I kicked the lock off the door, grabbed my stuff and moved on. I've never taken a heavy dose of Valium since. (JM, Bristol)

Stained

I'd taken six Valium on the bus ride from Delhi to Goa, hoping to sleep the whole way, but lay on my bag during the trip. The water bottle burst open and I woke up covered in black dye and soaking wet. Needless to say, my immediate concern was that the Valium hadn't kept me unconscious, so I ate the rest of the tray, another six. My friend had to carry me off the bus. We then spent a week in a hotel, the walls of which were covered in dubious-looking stains, taking a lot of acid and getting our heads together. (RB, London)

In Australia it's illegal to drive barefoot, for whatever reason: if you're caught driving without shoes on, you can get fined. Anyway, we were haring along some road in the outback, my friend with his nose in a bag of cocaine while I chased the dragon with some China White I'd scored a few days before. Suddenly my friend, who's driving, starts flapping his arms at me, thrusting his bag of cocaine towards my mouth and screaming, 'Take this!' But I've got a pipe in my mouth and I'm holding a square of foil, so I don't want it. 'Take it!' he repeats. 'The cops are right behind us! I've got to put my shoes on.' I put the baggie in my mouth and stash the rest of the gear under the dash, just as the cop car pulls us over.

'Do you have any idea how fast you were going?' asks the cop. We feign ignorance. He tells us we were going around 170 km an hour and slaps a $1,400 fine on us, which some-how we never got round to paying. Still, I couldn't believe that going that fast, with large amounts of hard drugs in the car, my friend was mainly concerned about not being caught driving barefoot! (TG, Brighton)

The Big Score

I was sitting on a bench in the central square in Cali, Colombia, when a man approached me. 'You want to buy some weed?' he asked. I was game: I'd just come from a small town where it seemed that everyone and his dog smoked, and the weed had been good and dirt cheap. We haggled for a while, then I arranged to buy an ounce for some ludicrously low rate. He told me to wait there; he'd be back soon. I suppose I should have seen the warning signs, but I didn't: I just sat there like a chump. When he came back he took me on a weaving journey around loads of back streets, until we finally ended up in a café. I didn't have a clue where we were. There was nobody else in the café. We sat at a table, and he handed me a small amount of weed. At first I refused to take it. 'That's not an ounce!' It was barely an eighth. We haggled for a while, but he seemed insistent that I take it, eventually telling me he'd just give it to me for free. This seemed reasonable, so I took it – and all hell broke loose.

Armed soldiers in full camouflage gear emerged from the back of the café and handcuffed us both to our chairs. My dealer was babbling now: 'Don't arrest me! I'll pay you anything! A thousand dollars!' He didn't fool me – the whole thing was an obvious con to extract panic cash from the gringo. But that didn't mean I wasn't panicking. A couple of men in dark suits oozed from the shadows and targeted me.

'You don't want to go to jail, do you?' I shook my head. 'You have to pay them – a thousand dollars, or you go to jail.' I shook my head again and told them that I didn't have a thousand dollars. All I had was a hundred dollars – which I'd just taken out of the bank, and which I knew they'd find when they searched me. I told them to take that. They were not impressed. What did I have in my room? Did I have a credit card? They'd take me to a cashpoint now and make me take out the thousand dollars.

I told them that I had nothing in my room, not even a camera, and that I'd taken the hundred dollars out earlier that day; that was my limit for the day, and I wouldn't be able to take any more out. It wasn't true, but it worked. Reluctantly, they let me go and told me to fuck off. I left, my ears burning with shame at having walked into such an obvious trap, the dealer still babbling about unreasonable sums of money behind me. (JM, Bristol)

Gold-plated Gun

I'd just arrived in Santo Domingo, Dominican Republic, for the carnival. I was with two friends and we'd gone to a casino for a while, but we were kicked out when they realised we weren't going to spend any money. When we came out the streets had gone apeshit: the Dominican Republic had just won the Caribbean baseball championships, and it was street party time. People were driving around dragging fridges behind their cars, everyone dancing in the streets, fire hydrants busted open, that kind of thing. My two friends went back to the hotel to get their video cameras, and while they were away I was approached by a couple of hookers. I'd seen them earlier; when we were in a café before going to the casino, one of my friends had been chatting to them, and they'd eyed me up then. They were coming on strong now, and told me they had some coke. If I wanted to have a good time with them, all I'd need to do would be to pay for the coke. Sounded good to me.

We tried to go back to my hotel first, but the owner wouldn't let us in. No problem, says one of the girls – I know just the place. And they took me on a walk through the back streets of the city, past the cemetery; all dark roads, which were starting to spook me a little. Then a car pulled up in front of us, and five men got out. One was holding a gold gun; all were dressed in casual clothes. The girls ran off screaming, and the man with the gun put it to my head. He told me he was a policeman, and bundled me into the car, which then pulled away. I had a small bundle of weed on me, and I was trying to take it out of my pocket and stuff it down the back of the car seat – but then I realised that these weren't cops. Or if they were, they were definitely bad cops.

I gave them my moneybelt. It had everything in it. My passport, travellers cheques, Visa card, cash – all my valuables. The car stopped by a ditch. There were no street-lights here at all, and I was sure that I knew what was going to happen now. It was like it happened in slow motion. They unlocked the door and I opened it, stepping out and fully expecting to feel the bullet in my skull. And then it all sped up again, and I was running, weaving around the blocks, back towards the street party. I hid every time I saw a car I thought might be theirs, petrified that they'd come back to finish the job. But finally I made it back to my friends. (RB, London)

A German 'tourist', supposedly on a golf holiday, showed up at customs with his golf bag. While making idle chatter about golf, the customs official realised that the tourist did not know what a 'handicap' was. The customs official asked the tourist to demonstrate his swing, which he did – backwards. Narcotics were found in the golf bag.

7. I'M WITH STUPID

Holidaymakers may remember to take their passports with them, but they often leave their brain cells behind. The following stories reveal just how badly some tourists wrong-foot themselves when they leave home.

Wandering alongside Cardiff Castle I was accosted by a middle-aged American couple who, I kid you not, were wearing tartan EVERYTHING (obviously their family was Scottish in the mid-1800s or something). They pointed at the Welsh flag flying majestically over the castle and asked, 'Is that some sort of family emblem?'

I just smiled, weakly. (PH, Cardiff)

While staying in a bed and breakfast in Bath a few years back, we overheard two American couples very proudly and very loudly reviewing their travel itinerary for the benefit of everyone else in the room. They were, however, stumped on the terminology of one of the books, which was describing the 'quintessential' English village. So, after much consultation among their table, they determined that as 'quint' means five, and 'essential' means necessary, that the village must be 'five times more important than other villages'. (MC, Anaheim)

In England, the walk/don't walk signs emit sounds, alerting people when it is and is not safe to walk. During a Guide Friday bus tour in Bath, an American woman asked the guide about the sounds. He replied that it was for the safety of the blind. Her reply: 'My God, y'all let the blind drive over here!' (MC, Anaheim)

While visiting Stonehenge with my family, I overheard an American couple talking (loudly) about how they believed that Stonehenge was brought down and placed there by a glacier. (PH, Cardiff)

During a stay in Rome I was eating lunch in a restaurant near the Vatican Museum, which was always overflowing with tourists, when an American couple walked in and sat at the other end of the restaurant. This was not far enough away; from the moment she received the menu, the wife kept saying to the waiter in louder and louder tones, 'What's this, what's this?' All this when the menu was written in four languages; Italian, French, German and ENGLISH! (DW, Dallas)

Our experience came while standing in the ticket line to go to the top of the Eiffel Tower. An American man with a child was in front of us. We overheard him asking for free admission to the top. She politely said no, in English, and the

American began to plead. She quoted the guy the price and then he yelled (so that everyone could hear), 'What is wrong with this stupid place, not letting me go for free. Do you know who I am? I'm an American! If it weren't for me, you wouldn't be here today. We saved your country. We should at least get something for free!' and he walked away saying 'stupid country'. (IM, Sacramento)

A large cruise ship pulled in to Gizo in the Solomon Islands. The passengers were treated to a totally plastic dance display by non-Solomon Islanders, then headed off to the hotel for a drink. Just about every artist/carver for miles around had come down from their villages with their artwork, and one elderly American couple stopped to buy something. The woman, clutching her purchase, screamed in anger at her husband, 'He won't take my credit card! Stupid man, doesn't he know we only pay by credit card? What can I do?' Then she threw the item back and stalked off, grumbling really loudly about the stupidity of the people, and why didn't they cater to tourists? I was so embarrassed to be seen in white skin, I hid. (JH, Toronto)

We made reservations for the train from Florence to Rome, but two other Americans were already in our seats. My husband and another gentleman went to get a conductor to settle the issue.

The conductor arrived just as the train was leaving. We all provided our reservation cards and the conductor informed the other Americans that they should have got off at Florence. One of them responded that they had not yet arrived in Florence, but the conductor pointed out that we had indeed just left Florence. The gentleman spluttered, 'What do you mean Firenze is Florence?' The conductor pointed to their tickets which showed Firenze as their stop.

The gentlemen then demanded that they stop the train and let them off, but this was a non-stop train to Rome. They even argued with the conductor that they should not have to pay a fine as Florence was not clearly stated as the stop. This train was full and they were forced to stand the entire way to Rome, roughly two hours.

The former occupants of our seats glared at us throughout the trip and complained loudly, 'The younger generation has no respect for their elders' and hinted that we should offer our seats. (We are in our thirties. They were in their forties.) But both my husband and I were sick with the flu and hoped to sleep on the train, and the Italian couple across from us rolled their eyes and whispered, 'Stupid Americans. Stay in seats.' So we stayed. (SW, San Diego)

I saw an American couple go up to the Swiss Guard on duty near the Gate of the Bells (to the left of the Archbasilica). The yank bloke crossed the barrier and, despite the Guard yelling 'Alto! Stop! Halten-sie!', the bloke marched up to the guard and tried to pose with him while his wife took a picture! The guard (wisely) seized the tourist by the arm and hustled him through the archway, out of sight. The guard then assumed a new stance outside the hut, effecting a new defensive posture. Soon, two more Swiss guards in navy fatigues joined him.

After about half an hour, during which the man's wife sobbed, wailed, and threatened to go to the US embassy, he finally emerged, escorted by four or five of the Vatican officials. They were taken to the Italian border near the via del Consolazione. I followed, and heard them give the couple a lecture about respecting barriers. What a pair of dumbasses! You don't mess with the Pope's police! (HD, Exeter)

The Canning Stock Route in Central Australia is considered by four-wheel drive enthusiasts to be one of the most challenging routes on the planet. Most people who attempt the route plan far ahead, taking a number of spare tyres and a large amount of water – there are few facilities on the 1,700 km route to stock up on either essential, and being stranded usually results in death. Locals were mystified therefore when a German tourist was found bogged down by Lake Disappointment with ten litres of beer and no water and no communications equipment. He was fortunate to be found by a group of tourists who gave him water and alerted the authorities, who found him drinking the salt water from the nearby lake, having been stranded for three days.

In 1990, I was with a small group of people in Sarawak (Malaysian Borneo), where we were staying with some local Iban tribesmen at their longhouse. The guide was fluent in Bahasa, and I knew a little bit of it also, so we were the only two in the group who could communicate with the local people. At a boat launch on a local river, a member of our group, a woman from New York City, got very angry at an older local man because she wanted to buy something from him but he would not accept her credit card. The fact that he could not understand her just made her scream more loudly. The poor man had probably never seen a credit card before and did not know what it was. By the way, this was in a very remote area where they did not get many visitors. (EW, Dundee)

Lost in Space

In Dover in 1987, an English couple decided to cross the Channel in their motorhome and spend a few days in Paris. Unfortunately they totally forgot to take a map with them. They got lost in France as soon as they got off the boat and continued driving, without asking directions until they found themselves near the Swiss border. They then realised they were in the wrong place and headed back to Paris, this time driving through Luxembourg then into Belgium and Holland, thinking that they had to pass through these countries to get back to Paris. Eventually they arrived in Rotterdam and, thinking they had finally found the right road, they ended up in Bonn, Germany. They eventually ran out of money and had to beg for petrol money, returning to Dover a week later than they expected and driving over 1,000 miles non-stop.

In the French Alps, two Australian tourists were driving their clapped-out Vauxhall car while attempting to cross into Italy.

The roads were covered in snow and the tourists had neglected to buy snow chains for their tyres. This resulted in a traffic jam five miles long behind them. To keep their car from sliding over the edge to a certain death, they had to drive at five miles per hour, causing the drivers behind them to force them off the road into a side road. Unable to turn around, they had to wait six hours to be rescued by police who escorted them back to France.

In August 2003 three Italian tourists arrived in Dublin for a short holiday. After checking in to a hotel on the outskirts of the city, leaving their passports and airline tickets behind, they drove into town for a meal. It was only once they'd eaten their fill that they realised they had no idea where they were staying. They spent two days sleeping in their car, trying to make the most of their holiday and even following the rest of their travel itinerary, despite having lost their belongings. A Garda spokeswoman said: 'All they knew was that the accommodation might have had a green door, was on a main street and beside a school. They knew it was on the outskirts of the city but they didn't know if it was north or south and couldn't remember crossing a river.' The tourists were reported to be 'anxious to get their belongings back'.

A French girl on holiday in the UK for the first time found it difficult to cope with the vagaries of the M25, London's orbital motorway. She only needed to go fourteen miles, but after she'd missed her junction, rather than taking the next exit and turning around, she ended up driving all the way round the M25, all 120 miles, to get to her destination.

The View from the Inside

The following stories are supplied by tour operators, keen at last to have their revenge on particularly lunk-headed guests. Paint them black:

A visitor to Orlando returned from his holiday and called his tour operator in a rage. He had been expecting a sea-view room, and demanded to know why one had not been provided. The operator explained calmly to him that as Orlando is in the middle of the state of Florida, providing a sea-view room would have been impossible. 'Don't lie to me,' the angry tourist snarled. 'I looked on the map, and Florida is a very thin state.'

A man checking in for a flight to Spain asked if he could carry a fairly large bag on to the plane as hand luggage. The check-in staff noticed that it had a wire sticking out of it, so they asked him what it was.

'My TV,' he replied.

'Why do you want to take your TV on holiday?'

'We're playing Real Madrid on Wednesday, and I want to listen to John Motson, not some Spanish commentator. So I'm taking my TV.'

Apparently soap addicts routinely turn up at Heathrow and Gatwick with their TVs before hopping on a plane to Spain or Florida, desperate not to miss the next episode of their favourite programme. Perhaps nobody has ever explained to them how a TV works . . .

On disembarking from his cruise ship in Barbados, a tourist approached an immigration official and asked him a question he'd obviously been agonising over for some time: did the island have water all the way around?

On a trek in the Andes, one tour group member started to panic about altitude sickness, asking the guide if it would affect him more because he was the tallest member of the group. Similarly, a tour group member in the Himalayas worried about altitude sickness as he came from Norfolk.

A travel rep in Rio was alarmed to be asked by a member of the group he was looking after what altitude they were at. They were standing on the beach at the time.

On safari in Africa, a tourist asked a ranger if giraffes hunted in packs. When the ranger told her that all the giraffes he was familiar with were vegetarian, she threatened to report him for 'winding her up'.

At the end of her holiday, an enraged American woman called up her tour operator and demanded to know if physical descriptions were put on passengers' luggage so that staff could identify the owners of specific items. The operator told her that they were not, and asked why she wanted to know.

'Well, when I checked in with the airline, they put a tag on my bag that said FAT, and I'm overweight. Is there any connection?' The operator asked her a few further questions, and eventually it emerged that she had flown to Fresno, for which the airport code is indeed FAT.

Easy Marks

From licking the narcotic-coated nipples of Thai girls to buying bogus gems from 'state-approved' shops, tourists around the world often fall victim to a wide range of scams and cons. Away from their familiar environments, keen to experiment and lured by the idea of making some easy cash, many tourists make easy marks – and some betray a degree of gullibility far beyond the norm, as in the following stories:

In October 2002 a Zimbabwean man was arrested near Harare after allegedly disguising himself as a ghost and robbing tourists at a historic site elsewhere in the country. Police said the man worked naked with his body daubed in ash, and reported that he had stolen goods and money worth around £232,000 over a four-year period from tourist visitors to the Great Zimbabwe monument, an ancient stone structure. Some tourists were reported to have believed the 'ghost' to be the protector spirit of the monument, incensed at the steady stream of visiting foreigners.

In April 2002 four men – from Kenya, Liberia and Guinea –

were charged with conning an American tourist in Bangkok into buying £20,000 worth of black paper. They had told the American the paper, in dollar-sized pieces, was money that had been stained black in order to smuggle it out of Nigeria. If the tourist later bought a special chemical he could 'clean' the money, which would then be worth $900,000; but police, acting on an independent tip-off, arrested the four men before the tourist could be duped into spending further money on the chemical.

This scam has become very popular in the last few years, with a large number of tourists and business travellers approaching police to report that they have been ripped off while attempting to buy the 'cleaning' chemical – many find it difficult to accept that the 'black money' is in fact worthless paper. The con men characteristically use sleight of hand techniques to exchange a piece of black paper in a suitcase full of similar notes for a dollar bill, demonstrating the efficacy of the 'cleaning' chemical. Alternatively some notes inside the suitcase may in fact be dollars, stained with a mixture of Vaseline and iodine, which can be cleaned with ordinary cleaning fluid, while others will simply be black paper.

The 'black money' scam is said to be based on a centuries-old traditional West African con called the 'Red Mercury' scam. Rumours circulate around Internet sites that there is indeed 'black money' in Africa, stained by the leaders of corrupt regimes in an attempt to make it worthless currency to anyone else and indeed to export it undetected; a genuine 'cleaning' chemical is said to be available from a private Swiss consortium which demands ten per cent of the value of the money cleaned – with a minimum amount of $3 million to be cleaned. Potential investors would probably be wise to ignore this and indeed to avoid any scheme involving smuggled currency, Nigeria, and advance fees.

Ask a Silly Question

Tourist offices all over the world have to deal on a daily basis with bizarre and often frankly stupid requests. Here are some of the more choice questions asked by visitors to England:

- 'What time do the UFOs fly, where can we sit and watch them and would it be all right to bring a picnic?' (Todmorden Tourist Information Centre [TIC], West Yorkshire)
- 'I understand there is a gorilla-breeding establishment somewhere in the south of England. Please could you tell me where it is because I want to take my wife as a surprise?' (Sleaford TIC, Lincolnshire)
- 'What time does the Lake District open?' (Carlisle Visitor Centre, Cumbria)
- 'Can I change my English currency into Scottish currency?' (Carlisle Visitor Centre, Cumbria)
- 'Did Hadrian really build Hadrian's Wall?' (Carlisle Visitor Centre, Cumbria)
- 'Would you show me on the map exactly where the Scottish accent stops and the English accent starts?' (Carlisle Visitor Centre, Cumbria)

- 'What time does the 10.20 bus run?' (Todmorden TIC, West Yorkshire)
- 'I want to go somewhere north of Wales, and no, I don't want coastal areas, I want seaside!' (Sleaford TIC, Lincolnshire)
- 'I want to have a balloon flight/try gliding/hire a teddy cake-tin/try go-karting/watch the greyhound racing/get married in a beautiful location/play paintball/do off-road racing/have a murder mystery weekend/go to a health farm. Help!' (Oxford Information Centre, Oxfordshire)
- 'Where do I get the topless bus from?' (Oxford Information Centre, Oxfordshire)
- 'Is Dorking something English people do?' (question asked by a visitor after looking at the Dorking mini guide, Royal Tunbridge Wells Information Centre, Kent)
- 'How many fish are there in the sea?' (Brighton and Hove Visitor Information Centre, Sussex)
- 'Can you tell me where the Evening Mystery Tour goes?' (Weymouth TIC, Dorset)
- 'What do we do if we want to launch a boat and the tide is out?' (Weston-super-Mare TIC, Somerset)
- 'Where do we find houses with straw hats?' (Stow-on-the-Wold TIC, Gloucestershire)
- 'What day is the New Year's Day parade on?' (Britain Visitor Centre, London)
- 'Can you tell me why they built Windsor Castle on the Heathrow flight path?' (Britain Visitor Centre, London)
- 'I've got a squirrel in my kitchen and it's doing a lot of

damage. Can you come and get it out?' (Barnard Castle TIC, Co Durham)

Visitors to Scotland demonstrated similarly brain-burned needs:

- Tourists at a tourist information centre (TIC) in the Highlands asked staff how the snow got up Ben Nevis.
- Staff in Edinburgh were baffled by requests to know when the penguins left the zoo.
- A visitor to one TIC demanded to know, 'Is there anyone here who speaks Australian?'
- A visitor to Glasgow asked TIC staff 'Where are the northern lights and what time do they get switched on?'
- One tourist in the Highlands wanted to know if Fort William was still alive.

It's not only Tourist Information Centres that have to field this kind of question. Booking holidays also provides a fertile field for foot-in-mouth disasters:

- A man booking himself a cabin on a cruise asked if an outside cabin, described in the brochure as coming 'with porthole', was above sea level. Another customer also booking himself on a cruise called to ask if the portholes had glass in them. Both questions pale in comparison however with the young lady on a Voyages of Discovery cruise who asked a crew member what time the midnight buffet was served.

- A woman rang a tour operator to ask what temperatures she could expect on her Greek-island holiday. On her question being answered, she replied a little huffily, 'Well if that's the case I'm going with Thompson. It's hotter if I book with them.'
- A customer attempting to book a flight to Amsterdam demanded to know why it took over two hours to get there and just ten minutes to get back. She refused to buy the agent's patient explanation about time zones.
- A woman booking a flight to Australia with a travel agent requested a seat over the black box. When she was asked why she would like to sit there, she replied that it had to be the safest place on the plane, as the black box was always found in the event of an accident.
- Actually, maybe that's not such a bad idea ... and nor is this: on a returned holiday booking form under the listing for 'special dietary requirements', a canny traveller wrote 'No Brussels sprouts'.

Tourists in the USA demonstrated a similar lack of mental acuity, as shown by these visitor requests for information from a TIC in Death Valley, California. Death Valley is the lowest point in the Western hemisphere; it is notorious for its high temperatures during the day and receives less than two inches of rain a year:

- 'Can I buy cows in Death Valley?'
- 'Do you have camels for rent?'

- 'Can I rent snow skis at Furnace Creek? How is the skiing?'
- 'Please send me information on Hollywood.' (a request from Europe)
- 'Send me information on rafting trips in Death Valley.'
- 'Can we sleep in the sand in Death Valley?'
- 'Please send information about speedboat racing in Death Valley.'

US travel agents fielded similar queries, such as the following:

- 'I got a call from a woman who wanted to go to Cape Town. I started to explain the length of the flight and the passport information when she interrupted me with, "I'm not trying to make you look stupid, but Cape Town is in Massachusetts." Without trying to make her look like the stupid one, I calmly explained, "Cape Cod is in Massachusetts; Cape Town is in Africa." Her response . . . click.
- 'I got a call from a man who asked, "Is it possible to see England from Canada?" I said, "No." He said, "But they look so close on the map." '
- 'I had someone ask for an aisle seat so that his or her hair wouldn't get messed up by being near the window.'
- 'A client called in inquiring about a package to Hawaii. After going over all the cost info, she asked, "Would it be cheaper to fly to California and then take the train to Hawaii?" '
- 'A woman needed to know how it was possible that her flight from Detroit left at 8.20 a.m. and got into Chicago at

8.33 a.m. I tried to explain that Michigan was an hour ahead of Illinois, but she could not understand the concept of time zones. Finally I told her the plane went very fast, and she bought that!'

- 'A man called and asked if he could rent a car in Dallas. When I pulled up the reservation, I noticed he had a one-hour lay over in Dallas. When I asked him why he wanted to rent a car, he said, "I heard Dallas was a big airport, and I need a car to drive between the gates to save time."'

- 'A businessman called and had a question about the documents he needed in order to fly to China. After a lengthy discussion about passports, I reminded him he needed a visa. "Oh no I don't, I've been to China many times and never had to have one of those." I double-checked and sure enough, his stay required a visa. When I told him this he said, "Look, I've been to China four times and every time they have accepted my American Express."'

- 'One customer I spoke to asked, "How do I know which plane to get on?" I asked him what exactly he meant, to which he replied, "I was told my flight number is 823, but none of these damn planes have numbers on them."'

- 'A woman called and said, "I need to fly to Pepsi-cola on one of those computer planes." I asked if she meant to fly to Pensacola on a commuter plane. She said, "Yeah, whatever."'

- A woman called a travel agent to make a reservation, telling the agent, 'I want to go from Chicago to Hippopotamus, New York.' The agent was at a loss for words, and finally asked, 'Are you sure that's the name of the town?'

'Yes, what flights do you have?' replied the customer.

After some searching, the agent came back with, 'I'm sorry, ma'am, I've looked up every airport code in the country and can't find a Hippopotamus anywhere.'

The customer retorted, 'Oh, don't be silly. Everyone knows where it is. Check your map!'

The agent scoured a map of the state of New York and finally offered, 'You don't mean Buffalo, do you?'

'That's it! I knew it was a big animal!'

8. CRASS AND CRASSER

Promoters of international tourism like to kid themselves that tourists are all cultural ambassadors for their countries, keen to experience a little of what it feels like to live in a foreign community, and to use this experience to enrich their lives. Sadly this couldn't be further from the truth. Many tourists are inescapably crass individuals with scant respect for their hosts and exceedingly poor personal hygiene. Just because they have money in their pockets does not mean they should be treated as royalty. As it happens, they're probably more likely to end up being mugged . . .

I drunkenly stumbled along the Brazilian beach, looking for a suitable place to relieve the pressure of numerous caipirinhas and beers building up in my bladder. I saw a tree stump poking out of the sand and decided it would be as good a place as any to answer the call of nature. I wandered up to it, unzipped my trousers, modestly checked to ensure no one was around and pulled out my wanger ready to let fly all over the tree stump. Then a strange thing happened – the tree stump seemed to move, divide into two shapes and then speak.

Puzzled I peered down into the gloom and to my horror saw the tree stump was actually a courting couple sitting on the beach and looking up at me, terrified by the sudden and dreadful sight of a tall, red-haired, English madman muttering and standing over them with the apparent aim of either urinating on them or dumbly suggesting sexual gratification. They held each other tightly – an embrace that no doubt had been of passion seconds ago but which was now grim comfort in the face of such alarming adversity.

I shrieked and made the only dignified move my instincts could allow – I took flight. Unfortunately that lasted for about five metres when I was painfully stopped dead in my tracks, thrown in the air and ended up spread-eagled and suspended on a barbed-wire fence, helplessly caught by my hair, my clothes and the skin of my face. The couple stared wide-eyed as I babbled incoherently, trying to apologise in Portuguese that in my panic then disintegrated into a mixture of French, English and, finally, Spanish. In the long and many seconds it took to disentangle myself from the barbed wire I was also dimly aware that my cock was still hanging out, albeit desperately trying to retreat to safety of its own accord.

The next few days I walked round the island with a cap pulled low over my scratched face: luckily I never saw them again or else they took great care to avoid me. (AC, Glasgow)

I was in Slovakia for a wedding. The groom was the cousin of a guy from my home town, and his family had decided to invite us. On the Friday night before the wedding there were six of us out in one of the small pubs having a good laugh and enjoying a three-way language conversation.

Across from us there was a table of about five Germans being very loud and taking advantage of the very cheap beer with some obnoxious behaviour. They started talking shit about Slovaks, what they would like to do with some of the women in town, the people at our table, and so on. Of course one of our friends was Austrian and totally understood what they were saying.

The Germans decided to order some food, then one of the barmen came up to our table and one of the Slovak guys told him what these Germans had said about them. The barman then went out to the kitchen staff and passed on the message to them. Later two of the Germans' faces were very red as they'd put the hottest paprika and chilli in their meal. But we didn't find out the best thing until we saw the barman the next day at the wedding. Before they cooked the meat the chef had pulled down his pants and rubbed his balls against it, then cooked it, threw it on the floor, and then jumped from a chair onto the meat before serving it on the plate. (HW, Düsseldorf)

I was in Dresden, Germany, on a year-long exchange, and a German friend finally persuaded me to go to McDonald's with her. I started chatting with the two American women in front of us in line. Boy do I wish I hadn't. They asked me all kinds of questions about Dresden and my exchange, which I didn't mind, but then they asked me about my friend. 'Oh, she's German? You have German friends? That's so cute!' I wanted to die. (JE, Minnesota)

In Malia in the summer of 2003, there was a bunch of us drinking in a crowded apartment where the hotel manager didn't want any guests. At about 6 a.m. there's a banging on the door. We know it's the manager, so Papa G shouts, 'Fuck it!', drops his trousers and pants and runs towards the door, then stands there bollock naked while the embarrassed manager makes his excuses and leaves! (SB, Swansea)

My mate Jack was sharing a room in Thailand with two other mates. After going out for some beers and then going home, they wake up in the middle of the night to see him standing on the end of his bed, obviously not quite sure where he is, pissing onto the floor.

Later that holiday, he'd gone out for the night and wet his pants so badly that he'd had to nick someone else's shorts from a washing line and get changed. Unfortunately for him, he'd been seen doing this by a local Thai bloke, who thought it would be funny to tell the two girls Jack was trying to impress the next night. (MM, London)

One from Venezuela: we hiked up to some hot springs near Merida. Many local families were also bathing in the pool and picnicking with their children. Then a Dutch sports team arrived – couldn't work out if they played soccer or rugby – wearing shiny sports suits. They were really loud and obnoxious, not to mention badly dressed. And then, as if their clothes weren't offensive enough, in front of everyone, half a dozen of them pulled down their pants and took pictures of each other with their arses bared. I have no problem with nudity, and in fact always go to nudist beaches, but there and then, in a Latin American country, in front of those families, it was just one of the most disgusting and disrespectful travel experiences I ever witnessed. Someone should have kicked their pale European butts! (BS, New York)

I was in a crowd of many locals and a couple of foreigners in a bank in Nairobi, waiting patiently for a teller to make an appearance and, as soon as she did, three Frenchmen barged their way from the back to the front of the line, demanding loudly and aggressively that the teller change their cash before anyone else. Most places in Nairobi aren't particularly service-oriented, service is slow and, bless her, she slowed down even more, eventually refusing to serve them by making up some excuse that they had to produce their passports, which they didn't have with them, and ended up closing the wicket. They left, even angrier than before, after us foreigners hurled snide remarks at them. Then the teller came back and put paid to the generalisation that Nairobi isn't service-oriented – at least as long as you are not in a hurry, or French. The local customers kept smiling at us and nodding their heads in appreciation, I guess, and even insisted that we go first. We didn't. (IJ, Durham)

I lived in the Commonwealth of Dominica for a while, and

saw a number of incidents, one involving a French family at a dive shop. They were large, and ran from about six years old up to about sixty: three generations. When they signed up to dive, the dive shop owner said the small child couldn't dive. The French matriarch became quite indignant, and stated, 'In France he can dive all he wants.' The dive shop owner said, 'Well, we are not in France.' The woman then replied, 'I know that, this is a dump, and France is beautiful.' (JC, Berlin)

Once I was on the riverboat heading to Wat Po, and I was near the back (standing), and three monks were sitting in the designated 'reserved for monks' seats. There were four seats available and they had occupied three of the four. Well, a large foreign lady decided she would sit in the fourth seat next to a monk. Everyone who saw this was horrified and one of the monks whispered to her that she wasn't allowed there, and this lady just got into such a huff! She took it as a personal attack and started to talk loudly, berate the monk and shake her head as if the monks were the ones at fault! Totally classless! I do believe that monks aren't even allowed to touch women, and so this was seen as a big 'no-no'. Of course the seat was clearly printed 'Reserved for Monks' – she was just plain rude! (TG, Liverpool)

Monks won't always put up with such treatment, and some have even taken to out-crassing the crass tourists:

I experienced the wrath of a Thai Buddhist monk travelling

through Malaysia. First, in the Kuala Lumpur bus terminal, he accosted a Malaysian passenger and made him load his heavy bags and boxes underneath the carriage. Whenever the fellow passenger would make a mistake while loading his bag, the monk would whack him with his cane and yell at him. Then he berated the man for not understanding English. Now, this man spoke very good English, yet the monk's English was difficult to understand.

Once on the bus, the monk didn't like his aisle seat and wanted to sit next to the window. He was a monk, so he couldn't run the risk of a woman touching him while walking down the aisle. That's understandable. But then, he started poking people with his cane to make them switch seats—all the while berating them and calling them stupid for their poor knowledge of English. I unfortunately ended up sitting next to him. As one man walked down the aisle, the monk theatrically fanned his face and wondered aloud, 'How can these people smell like this? It's disgusting. Malaysian people need to wash.' On the way to Melaka, he'd point at the houses with tin roofs and loudly proclaim, 'These people live like dogs. The Malaysians have no pride.'

Much to my dismay, he engaged me in conversation. I asked him if he had been to Angkor. He went almost psychotic. 'You should call it Angkor Wat. If you call it Angkor you are stupid. It is called Angkor Wat.' Well, there's more to Angkor than just Angkor Wat, but whatever.

He talked about his time living in New Orleans. 'There are too many niggers there. They are all lazy and thieves.' This went on for two hours non-stop – correcting people's pro-nunciation, calling people stupid, complaining about Malaysians, etc.

Finally we get to Melaka and I'm hoping to get on my way. He wants to stay in the same guesthouse as me, but he didn't want one with a Chinese name – only one with an English name. 'Chinese people don't know how to run hotels.' He ended up getting in the same taxi as me. He kept calling the driver stupid because he couldn't understand his English. The driver glared at me, but I was able to signal that I had nothing to do with this Thai monk.

We get to the guesthouse I'd chosen. I was in charge of investigating the rooms to see if he'd find them up to his standards. Of course, I came back and told him they would not be good enough for him. The Muslim guesthouse owner didn't know why I was discouraging a possible customer. She said she had a friend with a better room in another building and left to show him the way. I warned her that he was rude.

When she returned, she agreed that she was glad he was not staying in her particular guesthouse. She said he was the rudest man she'd ever met. He'd told her she was stupid and wrong for pointing with her thumb, instead of her finger! (OD, Poole)

I'm an Asian American and had the following experience in Thailand. I was at Grace's hotel one Saturday night around 3.30 a.m. with my friend Griffin to pump some more alcohol

118

into our system. We were seated just beside the door, sharing a table with two Thai girls. While Griffin was away chatting up some friends, one of the Thai girls sharing our table called out to a farang (Westerner) who happened to walk past. As the Thai girl was seated behind me, I leaned to my right to let that farang pass as he approached her. Guess what he told me, with his hand in a sweeping manner – he told me to 'Fuck off' and gestured to me to give up my seat!

'Fuck you!' The damn guy got a shock when I loudly greeted him back in his own 'language'! With a beer in one hand, he asked if I had a problem, or if I wanted one? I'm pretty small in size and as I'm an Asian it might have given him the guts to throw his weight around, but he chose the wrong guy. Being me, I told him yup, and asked him to make my day, and asked him why he told me to fuck off. And guess what his reply was? He said he wasn't talking to me! Ha Ha . . .

I was pretty heated up with this middle-aged coward, and the Thai girls were telling me 'jai yen yen, jai yen yen' (take it easy). Realising he had picked the wrong guy, he extended his hand and said, 'We are adults and we are here to have fun.' Ha ha . . . have fun with my dick man, piece of shit! Damn guy really deserved to be 'woken and shaken up' . . . and I hope he'll learn his lesson soon! (BC, Portland)

I'm an American and have witnessed quite a few examples of bad manners from tourists, but here is a recent favourite of mine. I was in Evora, Portugal, a couple of summers ago.

While dining in an Italian restaurant, a young couple from France, seated close to my table, got upset with the waiter. The waiter only spoke Portuguese, and the French couple only spoke French and English. The Frenchman was upset that he had received the wrong-shaped pasta. He had wanted rigatoni, but had been given ziti instead. (Honestly, how pathetic and trivial is that anyway?) I, someone who speaks English, French and Portuguese, offered to translate and help mediate the dispute. For some reason, this infuriated the Frenchman even more – I think he was embarrassed that the 'uncouth' American could speak the local language and he could not – and he just got louder and louder. His wife was now clearly embarrassed. The Frenchman then stormed into the kitchen with his plate, in order to confront the chef. He soon came out of the kitchen with a smile on his face. Later, the waiter brought him a new plate of pasta to his liking.

By the way, the waiter told me (in Portuguese) that the kitchen staff, who were by now rightfully insulted, had urinated into the Frenchman's food before serving it to him. Serves him right! (WB, Boston)

On a flight from Delhi to Kuala Lumpur there were two arrogant Indian men several seats ahead of me. They kept pressing the 'service' button over and over and over again. That in itself made me annoyed enough to want to knock their blocks off! But when they proceeded to call the poor flight attendant 'servant' (among other insults to this man), I was beyond angry. The flight attendant got right in their faces, pointed to his name tag and said in a *very* angry and upset tone, 'I have a name and it is not servant. It's Julian!' That shut them up for the rest of the flight, thank God! (SC, Somerset)

I am Anglo-Indian, and had a bad tourist experience in Jodhpur, India. I was staying at a guesthouse and was walking from my room downstairs. An Israeli woman (whom I had never met) yelled down to me to get her some toast and coffee, as if I worked there. Later on she asked me to get her something else. I should have told her to get off her fat butt and get it herself, but I kept my mouth shut. (DC, Romford)

In August 2002 I was in Hanoi, Vietnam, sitting eating breakfast in a restaurant/cheap backpacker hotel in the popular 'old' area of town. The owner (in his fifties) was behind the counter dealing with paying customers etc., and his very elderly mother was helping to clear the tables when she could; as well as them, the owner's wife and young daughter were there dealing with people's queries etc. An Israeli couple came in and talked to the owner – they were staying upstairs – and the Israeli bloke suddenly started shouting and pointing at the owner, screaming 'No, no, no, you fucking c***!' He completely lost it, stamping his foot and throwing his arms around, still screaming at the owner. The owner tried to explain something to him, keeping his face blank and his voice low, but again and again he was interrupted by this bloke pointing his finger right into his face and leaning over the counter top. Then the Israeli suddenly jumped up on the counter and punched the Vietnamese guy right in the head. His hat was knocked off and he gripped the counter to steady himself; again, he kept his own temper in check, took a moment to steady his voice and spoke again to the Israeli. The couple went to sit down at a table opposite me and started shouting abuse at the menu.

Everyone in the restaurant froze when this happened, with all the other backpackers in total shock – I felt so ashamed to be a foreigner/backpacker. The mother started to try and appease the Israeli guy, speaking in Vietnamese to him and the girlfriend. The wife went to her husband's side and the young daughter looked like she was about to burst into tears.

The Israeli girl never opened her mouth once and just dutifully followed her boyfriend around. The Vietnamese are Buddhists, and to touch a Buddhist's head is seen to be the worst insult as it's seen as the seat of the soul. The mother struck me as having seen violence by Westerners before, the way she was trying to placate the Israeli – and I have the utmost respect for the Vietnamese dad who, in front of his whole family, was assaulted by a demanding and hysterically violent foreigner . . . (CR, Edinburgh)

When we were kids in Norway, we used to hang around the docks waiting for the *Hurtigruten* to berth. It used to be the mail boat and it ferried people from the next settlement, but predominately it is now a tourist boat, especially in the summer, and very popular with fat, rich white Americans and Germans. They usually have a few hours in town before they go back onto the boat.

One particular day there were three of us – one a Sami (indigenous person), one a real Norwegian boy, and myself, a mixed-race guy – walking around. These three white Americans, probably in their early 60s, said in their loud nasally voices, 'I can't believe they have niggers up here, and also short Asian people too.' We were talking away in Norwegian, and then all of a sudden we heard that loud crap coming from these American mouths. We stopped and I said, 'Yes, we do have them here, and we speak English as well', then my Sami friend said, 'Yes, we are only eleven and probably speak it better than you ever will.' (OL, Oslo)

One of the worst experiences I had in a two-month tour of Europe this summer involved an elderly American couple on a tour of Neuschwanstein, the enormous 'fairy-tale' castle near Munich. As our tour group entered one of the smaller rooms in the castle, I (a black American) and a very nice Chinese guy from Singapore that I had met on the train there passed by two older white Americans.

The woman turned to stare as we walked in, and loudly declared to her husband (and the entire tour group) that we 'couldn't possibly be on the English tour'. And this was from a resident of the most ethnically diverse English-speaking nation in the world! (OS, San Francisco)

I walked across Japan's most famous Zen garden which has been expertly and perfectly raked for hundreds of years, thinking it was some kind of footpath. I was chased off by a most un-Zen-like priest, looking like I had raped his daughter. (RE, Cairns)

I was at Neuschwanstein and decided to take the carriage to the top. We shared the ride with a sixtyish couple from the States. Waiting for the ride to begin, the man says, 'How much of this Mickey Mouse Nazi money do you want to get going?' and 'C'mon Adolf, let's get the show on the road.' I was just a college kid at the time, but to this day I kick myself for not speaking up. (FB, Chicago)

Aswan '94. A thirtyish Italian mother enters the lobby of a mid-range hotel with her husband and two kids, dressed in a black string bikini! Classic – and so insensitive that I immediately filed the incident away as a perfect example of how not to behave abroad. (ER, Seattle)

I was pretty sad to see the following incident on a property outside Anjuna, Goa. We had all been dancing all night, taking drugs, drinking etc. – in the morning a woman appeared with her two young kids and started to circulate, seeing if anyone had anything for them: i.e. she was begging. One of the bigger male partygoers yelled in her face – and I quote – 'Fuck off!! We are having a party!' I hope she didn't understand the words, but the tone was indication enough; she left in tears. I left Goa that day. (TG, Liverpool)

124

One Night in Bangkok

I was on one of my usual trips to Bangkok; I go a couple of times a year. I met up with my Thai girlfriend but on that night it was the birthday of one of her work colleagues. So I was out with four girls. The loud comments coming from tourists all around us were stuff like 'How much is the one opposite you?', 'Can we have the little one before you?', and so it went on. I'm sure you can see how hard it was to ignore it when no amount of verbal reasoning was getting anywhere. (DE, Minnesota)

I had a bad experience last year from a bunch of drunken young Brits. I was in Silom village with my Thai girlfriend and some of her friends. We had ordered food and then the insults started. The idiots were trying to get off with some of the girls I was with. When my girlfriend went to the toilet she had to pass their table. On her way back one of the guys grabbed her and was groping her. I had to say something and he let her go. But the insults continued so I felt left with no choice: leave the restaurant or do something. But my girlfriend was clearly very upset and offended.

So I went back to the table and told them politely to cool it or I would have to do something, meaning get the restaurant management or call the police. But the main culprit took that as provocation and jumped up and took a wild swing at me. I am not particularly proud of what I did – I just gave him one return punch and broke his nose. His buddies didn't react badly, fortunately, and they left quickly. (IK, London)

I was having a drink at a bar in Phuket and wanted to be alone that evening, so no 'lady drinks'. A bunch of Aussies walked in and immediately started fondling the girls. Bar girls have to put up with this behaviour, so they merely smiled. One of the Aussies wanted to go one better, so he took out his dick and told a girl to give him a blow job. Not to be outdone, a second Aussie also exposed his dick and told another girl to perform a blow job on him. The poor girls were in tears. I walked out in disgust and was soon followed by a bunch of Japanese and other nationalities who exited that bar. (RG, Manchester)

When I popped into a go-go bar recently I was horrified to see a bunch of loudmouthed drunk Brits making this girl feel awkward (and I am a Brit). One guy had her on his lap and in a moment of good ol' British 'high spirits' decided it would be fun to force her head down on his crotch. The poor bargirl did the best to smile as waitresses stood around wondering what to do. (EM, London)

The Ghoul Pool

For some tourists, there is little to distinguish culturally sensitive sites from other attractions. A trip to Auschwitz is little different in their minds from a visit to the Torture Museums of Amsterdam – buy a ticket, go in, gawp at man's inhumanity to man, buy a postcard, leave. Of course, it was never going to be easy to open concentration camps to visitors, and officials at such sites have been less than blameless in their attempts to make the camps turn a profit: at Auschwitz, which takes 3,000 visitors daily, there are fast food stalls and postcards of barbed wire in the sunset for sale; and at an American Holocaust museum punters can buy, for just $39.95, miniature replicas of the cattle cars in which Jews, Gypsies, homosexuals and other Nazi-proscribed 'deviants' were taken to their death.

The following incidents give some idea of the characteristically gauche reactions to concentration camps as tourist attractions:

I was visiting a concentration camp in Germany. We were in a large movie room near the entrance where they were going to show a fifteen-minute video for visitors. I heard a bunch of American guys yelling to each other and whoever was sitting next to them – 'Anyone got popcorn? Anyone?' … I was ENRAGED. (EJ, Chicago)

While staying in Krakow I took a day-trip to the Nazis' largest and most infamous death camp. It was an overwhelmingly sombre, sobering, and thought-provoking experience. However, an American couple ignored the signs outside suggesting that the material may be too intense for children under twelve and brought their four-year-old daughter and their eight-year-old son along on the English language tour. At first I was a bit irritated by the kids – fidgeting, talking, and not paying attention to the guide – but then I realised that my real frustration was with the parents who didn't have enough sense to realise that their kids weren't old enough to appreciate the importance and the tragedy of the place and the respect it deserved.

As the tour went on, it became clear that the real problem was that the parents didn't 'get it' either – explaining brutal executions to their kids in sing-song voices as though they were exhibits at Disney World, loudly discussing their travel plans and accommodation while we were in the most powerful parts of the camp and, most unbelievably, having one of the kids pose for a picture with a sculpture of an emaciated woman commemorating the starvation of the victims. Everyone on the tour breathed a sigh of relief when they decided to leave the tour early. (TH, Orlando)

In July 2003 a 60-year-old German tourist was arrested after being caught trying to steal a crematorium door from the former Stutthof concentration camp in northern Poland. When he was stopped by guards he attempted to bribe them, then claimed that he had thought the door was scrap metal and had decided to take it to fit a building project at home.

In November 1999 a group of forty seventeen- and eighteen-year-old Israeli high-school students ended a week-long tour of Poland's death camps by inviting male and female strippers to their hotel rooms in Warsaw. Details of the incident emerged when the students returned to Israel, boasting of their exploits and showing photographs of the strippers entertaining them, some of which found their way into the

Israeli press. Efraim Zuroff, the director of the Jerusalem office of the Simon Wiesenthal Centre, told the press that 'After seven days of dealing with the most harrowing experiences, they are looking for some way to relieve the tension', although other Israeli commentators were less understanding.

9. CULTURE VULTURES

Some tourists intend to improve themselves on holiday by taking in cultural sights, including museums and art galleries, and sampling the delights of local cuisine. But no matter how good their intentions, some just can't seem to leave their cretinous assumptions and unsuitable behaviour behind ...

Overheard by an acquaintance while he was at the Roman Baths in Bath:
Middle-aged American female: 'Oh mah god, can you buh-leeeve they swam in that unfiltered water?' (IM, Bristol)

My most horrifying experience of witnessing stupid tourist behaviour involved an American girl who leaned forwards and actually scratched at the paint on Monet's *Waterlilies* to see how thick it was! (JK, London)

While I was attending a classical concert in Vienna, the elegant pre-curtain hush was broken by the exclamation: 'HEY MA!! LOOKAT THIS PLACE! WWHEW WEEEE!!!!! LOOKIE THAT CHANDELIER. DAMN THIS PLACE IS

PERTY!' A cowboy-hatted American family stumbled to their seats in the first row . . . (NB, Hull)

I was in the Rijksmuseum in Amsterdam at the same time as a large tour. These Americans talked so loudly that several other groups on guided tours in the museum could not hear the guides. They were told to shut up in several different languages. After that they complained loudly again that people were so rude in Holland. As they were leaving I heard one man wearing a 10-gallon hat say, 'Let's go to McDonald's to get some good food.' (AB, Portsmouth)

In Musee D'Orsay, with circular signs all over showing lines through flash cameras, a woman was taking pictures with a flash. I shot her an ugly look and her response, with an American twang, was, 'It doesn't turn off' – I shot back with 'guess postcards will have to do.' (CJ, Johannesburg)

Last May, two friends and I were having dinner at a fine restaurant in Monterosso, Italy. Behind us was a table of Americans, led by a loud, demanding older woman (who also happened to be staying at the same hotel as we were). She was from San Francisco and boasted of running a cooking school there. These other people with her were students on a cooking adventure.

Shortly after we were seated, we overheard her call the waiter over. She said, 'When I make this sauce, these are my ingredients . . .' and told him how his cook should have made the sauce. The audacity! She even demanded to see the cook in the kitchen! When the waiter wouldn't comply, she accused him of having a New York attitude (having overheard him tell us that his good English was from having lived in New York for a couple of years), and demanded to see the owner. He did a swirl and a low bow and when he stood up, he announced that he was, indeed, the owner!

That almost tongue-tied this woman, but not quite. She continued complaining about the food and the service and soon had her companions complaining as well. By the way, our food was wonderful! But then, we were open to experiencing the regional cuisine, not imposing our methods on them.

At last, I could stand no more, and told this woman that she had given me the best laugh of the day with her ridiculous behaviour, adding that I thought she should be ashamed to call herself an American, and I hoped that the rest of us would not be judged by her crowd's obnoxious behaviour. Well, after I said that, a couple sitting a few seats away from us began to applaud; they were from New York and were offended by the rude American's comment on the 'New York attitude!'

The owner was so grateful for our support that he brought out the lemoncella liqueur and passed it around our side of the veranda, free of charge. (SI, San Antonio)

I saw a young, pierced American couple posing for photos in an empty confessional, and then taking a photograph of a penitent confessing his sins. One of the young men who volunteers in the Archbasilica saw this, and called the gendarme on duty over. They escorted the young couple out (despite their protests that they were American, and that 'you can't kick someone out of a church') and cautioned them that if they returned again, they would be arrested. (TR, Coventry)

I saw a crass American tourist in London at the Victoria and Albert Museum. I wouldn't describe it as 'horrifying', but it made me uncomfortable. In the jewellery exhibit, an American woman insisted on commenting on every display at the top of her lungs: 'Now look at that necklace. Looks like they didn't know what colour to use so they used them all. Looks like Mardi Gras', and, 'Look at that coral. Whaddaya mean you don't like orange? You MUST love orange. I just don't understand you', etc. etc. But what really made me cringe was her parting comment: 'I just don't see anything inspiring here. I thought I was going to get some ideas for my bead projects at home, but it's just not gonna happen at this place!' I imagine it takes more than one of the finest collections of jewellery in the world to inspire 'bead projects'. She made my stomach hurt. (RW, London)

During the time I lived in Italy, my favourite ugly tourist sighting was at the Forum in Rome. My friends and I overheard a female (presumably American) tourist proclaim in a loud Southern accent: 'I don't understand what all this fuss is about, it's just a bunch of RAWCKS!' (JH, Bristol)

Overheard while viewing the Crown Jewels display, Tower of London: Young American female: 'So, like, what is it about them that, like, makes them so special?' (UT, Winchester)

While in Venice, I overheard an American woman lecturing our Italian hostess about her disappointment over the food in Italy: 'Have you ever tasted REAL Italian food? You know, the food you have here isn't even REAL Italian food! Do you KNOW where we can get some real Italian food?' Our Italian hostess did not speak English. She just smiled. The obnoxious American woman finally walked out in disgust. (DE, Cardiff)

At the Vienna Opera House gift shop after a tour of the opera house: An American man with a loud voice asks the sales clerk, 'I'm looking for a CD of opera music, but I've never really liked opera. Do you have anything you would recommend?' (RW, London)

While standing in the plaza in front of Notre Dame early one morning in Paris I overheard an older American man loudly asking a police officer, 'Where is this Noter Da-me place?' (IM, Bristol)

I was at the Edinburgh Military Tattoo a few years ago and when 'God Save the Queen' was played, the American tour group in front of us loudly sang 'My Country Tis of Thee'. One of the women asked her grandson if 'they still taught that song in school' and when he indicated that they did not, she said, 'Well, they ought to.' My wife and I thought this was hysterical. (TS, Manchester)

I found my 'favourite' ugly American at the Uffizi in Florence ... where there are signs everywhere forbidding flash photography. Me and about 5,000 other visitors were trying to enjoy da Vinci's *Annunciation*, when we were interrupted by a group of six big-haired American women. One whined loudly about how impossible it is to take a picture of the art because 'all of these people just won't get out of my way!' So before we knew what was going on, her little gang of five started pushing people out from in front of the painting, locked arms, and created a human barricade behind their leader, who then proceeded to take a flash photograph. It was mortifying. (SG, Mitcham)

I visited Rhodes last year. It's a stunning island, with incredible historic monuments and outstanding natural beauty. I'd heard of Faliraki but didn't want to go anywhere near it, not my scene at all. I know some people complain that those tourists don't go anywhere else on the island, but as far as I'm concerned they can stay in their resorts. I had one experience of contact with them and that was more than enough. It happened when I walked up to the ancient Acropolis at Lindos, a spectacular monument that's as impressive as anything else on the Greek islands. There was a group of young English louts coming up, all looking slightly the worse for wear. I avoided talking to them – in fact they made me feel ashamed to be British – but couldn't help watching when they got to the top. True to form, one of them was violently sick when they got there, much to the disgust of the other tourists and the guides, and the group egged him on. I overheard them afterwards talking about how much each of them had drunk, stupid quantities really. It's not the kind of image we want to export abroad, although it's probably a bit late to do anything about that – can't we just take their passports away? (RM, Dublin)

10. WHEN TOURISTS ATTACK

For many tourists, making official complaints when things go wrong isn't enough. They have fists, after all, and maybe glasses or bottles as well – why wait for a formal letter of apology when satisfaction can be obtained by a punch in the face?

When I was working at Epcot, I saw a group of Brazilian tourists accost Winnie the Pooh and Piglet when they came out for a character meet and greet. In the time it took Pooh's handler to go to the phone to call security and return, the group had dismantled a temporary queue and lashed Pooh to a lamppost using the ropes. (CW, San Antonio)

This is not an isolated incident at the Happiest Place on Earth. Disneyland visitors have been known to physically and verbally assault other tourists and cast members with increasing frequency over the past decade, especially during the summer months. If a visitor has paid around £30 to stand in the midday sun in a two-hour queue for a ride that lasts little longer than a minute – and may well break down just before he gets on to it – it's not surprising if his temper boils over.

While Disneyland does not publicise such outbreaks of rage, for obvious reasons, ex-workers have spilled the beans about what really goes on behind the smiley Mickey Mouse masks. A typical summer weekend will see around ten assaults, according to one ex-cleaner, ranging from violent scuffles in queues for the toilets to ride staff being slapped, punched or spat on. Security in the park has been scaled down substantially since it was criticised for being too harsh, and now an average summer day sees only two plainclothes officers on duty. As one uniformed guard put it, 'It's sad when you are keeping an eye on Snow White and a guest comments that you're the only security officer they've seen all day.'

One of the key conflagration points is the FastPass system, which allows visitors who have purchased tickets in advance to skip to the head of the normal queue at certain times of day. Many visitors are unaware of the system, and visitors taking advantage of FastPass tickets are routinely heckled by those in the standby queue; in some cases fights have broken out.

Staff working on the FastPass control points have historically had a high turnover rate, with some never returning after their first shift, disturbed by the inventive profanities hurled at them by irate holidaymakers. Nowadays most of the FastPass shifts are given to crew members who are considered more likely to be able to deal with being attacked both verbally and physically; some even stop the standby queues on a whim just to see how creatively they can be insulted. But even these hard men of the theme park circuit may have found it difficult to deal with the following incidents:

Cairo, 1994. Two tough-looking German men, one who was a young adult and the other who seemed to be his dad, started to really beat an innocent guide after he discreetly pointed out that they were on the wrong bus to the pyramids. Very ugly incident. (SL, Monmouth)

While I was sitting by the pool in a hotel in Sri Lanka a German guy had been on a three-hour boat trip and then refused to pay because he said his wife hadn't been comfortable! The boat trip guy (quite rightly) asked why he hadn't said he wanted to stop – and was getting angry but not at all violent. The German guy hit him and then called security to throw him out, but luckily his friends came to get him out before security got there. (JP, Reading)

This story was also in Sri Lanka and this time involved a Brit. A security guard who was only just learning new languages said 'good night' in German so the British bloke hit him! Apparently the only thing that stopped him getting 'a good kicking' was his wife threatening to leave him and screaming her head off. (I can't help but wonder if she got 'a good kicking' later on?) (JP, Reading)

In July 2003 a British family were arrested after allegedly beating the owner of a tourist shop so badly that he was left with a broken leg. The incident, which took place near the Acropolis in Athens, began when the shop owner complained at the sight of the family – comprising husband, wife and two sons – tracking food from the kebabs they had brought in all over the floor. Greek detectives claimed that the family used towels on sale to wipe the blood from the resultant scuffle from their hands and faces.

In August 2001 nineteen British families took a representative of their tourist company hostage to protest against the appalling conditions of their hotel in El Arenal, Mallorca. Among the conditions that had led them to take this drastic step were the presence of animal bones, used condoms and clothes floating in the filthy pool, ants in the hotel food, stale bread being served for breakfast and cockroaches in the bedrooms. One tourist told *The Times* that her family's room had contained three single beds with broken legs, a stool, one working lightbulb, no air conditioning and a thousand hungry and noisy mosquitoes.

The furious holidaymakers, after threatening to insert their suncream bottles into the holiday rep's rear, were finally persuaded to release him after a two-hour stand-off with police. A representative of the tour company in the UK told press that he had been assured by the hotel manager and the company's Spanish counterparts that the conditions were nowhere near as bad as had been made out. He added, 'We have not received complaints from other people we have booked into the hotel.' Well, maybe those weren't animal bones in the pool after all ...

Hooligan Holiday
Keep St George in my heart
Keep me English
Keep St George in my heart I pray
Keep St George in my heart
Keep me English
Keep me English till my dying day
No surrender
No surrender
No surrender to the IRA

The fame of the English football hooligan has spread far and wide. From the mountaintop monasteries of Nepal to the cloud forests of Guatemala, the eyes of locals who have never travelled more than a few miles from their place of birth will light up at the sight of an Englishman as they ask, 'Hooligan?' The country's most obnoxious national export isn't likely to go away any time soon – the sense of community given by such songs as 'No Surrender to the IRA', 'Stand up if you Hate Germans' and 'I'd Rather Be a Paki than a Turk' is too strong for that – but its more violent manifestations tend to be caused by media hype and over-policing nowadays, and the mantle of most violent football crew has been taken up by other countries.

Still, countries awaiting an influx of English football fans plan emergency manoeuvres as though expecting a terrorist atrocity. Before the 2002 World Cup held in Japan and Korea, Armageddon in the shape of football fans was feared to be descending soon, and anti-riot exercises were staged using locals dressed in England shirts. For added authenticity they should have used Burberry caps as well; not for nothing are the contemporary English hooligans known as the Burberry Brigade.

The heyday of English hooligan violence was the mid-70s to the late 80s. By then, the burgeoning rave scene had put paid to some of the worst excesses of terrace violence, as many casuals got heavily involved with Ecstasy and dancing. But before the firms started gurning they were a bloodthirsty lot, and incidents such as the following were not uncommon.

On 7 August 1986, a ferryload of football supporters sailed out of Harwich on their way to Holland to see Manchester United and West Ham play abroad. While most of these were simply fans of both sides intent on following their teams away, travelling in first class were fourteen faces from West Ham's notorious Inter City Firm (ICF), while propping up the bar were around 150 Manchester United lads.

The two sides had had a bitter rivalry since the 1960s, and it was only two hours before the inevitable confrontation took place. After the usual bout of verbal abuse and a brief skirmish, the outnumbered ICF faces took refuge in first class, where they grabbed whatever weapons they could – bottles, fire extinguishers, and even a fire hose on full blast – and manned all the stairs leading up from the lower decks, driving down the frustrated Manchester United fans.

As the fighting grew more and more intense, with decks and aisles slippery with blood, the captain sent out distress signals, decided the journey was too risky to be completed, and turned back to Harwich. On arrival the boat was met by a heavy police and media presence, with over twenty Manchester United fans requiring immediate hospitalisation.

Also travelling on the boat had been a group of Hell's Angels heading for a rally in Holland, who had refused to get involved; apparently the ICF were 'too violent' for them.

If such levels of violence are probably a thing of the past, indulgence in theft and vandalism is still very much in evidence. There is a long tradition among English fans abroad of spending as little money as possible en route to matches – or even making a profit. Trains can be bunked, tills looted and shops robbed of their produce, fans entering en masse and leaving with their pockets stuffed full of food and alcohol; the sheer weight of numbers leaves shop owners powerless to stop them. A similar ruse is employed in cafés, with many establishments on the Continent requesting payment of the bill only after goods have been consumed. This is seen by many fans as evidence of the stupidity of the foreigners, and the attendant ingenuity of the English in hoodwinking their hosts.

But some proprietors refuse to put up with such behaviour. In Brussels during the mid-1980s a café owner, incensed by watching a group of Tottenham fans eat his food, drink his beer and break his furniture then walk out without paying, pulled out a shotgun from behind the bar and shot a fan dead. It turned out later that he'd picked one of the few honest punters – the victim had paid his bill.

Looting occurs sporadically during riots, and organised shoplifting is not unknown, light-fingered fans exporting their talents to capital cities around the world. Sometimes the connections to organised crime are stronger: a Manchester-based operation during the 1980s printed fake American dollars for sale to football fans who would then travel to remote areas relatively unused to tourists to exchange the counterfeit funds.

Of course hooligans aren't the only tourists to indulge in criminal behaviour on holiday. Some tourists prey on others to finance extended stays abroad, using a variety of con tricks to part them from their cash, and tourists routinely leave hotels and restaurants without paying, or charge expensive consumer items to bogus hotel rooms. But while others may steal, hooligans still have the edge in vandalism:

Me and my mates used to follow England around on internationals, mainly for everything that went along with it, not just the football. You could travel pretty cheaply, just taking stuff from the supermarkets or smaller shops as you went, though we almost got nicked once, as we'd stuffed so much stuff down our front we couldn't give it legs like normal.

It was only fair to let people know we'd been in town, so we'd always leave a calling card. We'd go into a café or a bar, have some drinks, then one of us would go up to the toilet and stop and block it. What this means is he'd get into the cistern, take off the ballcock – most of them just unscrew – stop up the overflow pipe then lock the door and climb out. We'd leave, then sometimes go back the next day to see what had happened. A couple of times, with toilets upstairs, we managed to make the ceiling of the main room collapse. A bit of a giggle, but we got chased by one of the owners once who saw us come back and worked out what had happened. (GM, Southport)

And if you want to avoid a good kicking, you're better off not hanging out in any sports bars on holiday:

I'd gone out to Benidorm with a few mates – we'd got a cheap deal at the last minute, towards the end of the summer, but there were still loads of people there. Obviously we went out and got pissed a lot, but there was one night when we got really trashed, which just happened to be the night England were playing a friendly international. We went to a sports bar that was showing it, full of English people. One of my mates was wearing an Arsenal top and I was wearing a Bournemouth top, and I was getting all kinds of dirty looks from some people sitting on another table, who were all wearing Southampton tops. There's no love lost between Bournemouth and Southampton supporters, and while I don't think there was any trouble there and then, I was probably giving them the eye a bit as well.

It all gets a bit blurry from here on in – I ended up getting separated from my mates and meeting a girl. She was really nice, came back to the hotel room and we spent the night together, even swapped numbers in the morning and I've arranged to see her back in England. That was all fine, but in the morning she asked me if I'd seen my shirt. I was like, 'No?' and she said, 'It's got a few marks on it.'

So I had a look, and it turns out the bottom's covered in blood. I realise that my fingers are a bit cut, but they aren't bleeding. Not any more, anyway. They're clean cuts, like you get from broken glass. I check out my trousers, and find out they're covered in blood. There's no way my fingers could have bled that much, and although I don't remember exactly what happened, I reckon after I'd got split up from my mates the Southampton supporters tried it on, and I must have glassed one of them. I would have avoided the bar where it probably happened, if only I could remember where it was! And God knows why the girl thought I was a safe bet, covered in blood. (PH, Bristol)

11. BAD AIR DAY

Air travel is child's play, a recent ad campaign for a leading airline told us. How very apposite: bullying, brawling, random slinging of faecal matter and absurd tantrums are features linking air travel to child's play all too clearly. Next time you fly, remember not to drink too much, take any drugs, abuse other passengers or punch stewardesses – and never, ever, take a dump on the food trolley.

During a February 2000 flight to Toronto a woman was described by police as threatening to 'kick the ass of a female passenger' before stealing food off another passenger's meal tray, drinking and lighting cigarettes then being sick on herself. Neighbouring passengers demanded to be moved to other seats, and one was quoted as saying that he'd 'never seen such loud and disgusting behaviour'.

On a holiday flight from London to Florida a 56-year-old grandmother, described in court as 'of impeccable character', got drunk and inhaled 'poppers' (amyl nitrate) with a drag artist sitting next to her. She then became abusive, and tried three times to hit a stewardess who asked her to sit down and fasten her seatbelt as the plane prepared to land. She was so drunk when the passengers disembarked that she had to be taken off the plane in a wheelchair, but even then she continued to lash out and swear at cabin crew and US customs officials. She told police later that she believed her drinks had been spiked by the drag artist sitting next to her, and that she couldn't remember anything between having her first few drinks and waking up hours later on the floor of the US immigration office. She was jailed for six months.

While on a United Airlines flight a stewardess was serving food from the meal trolley. A female passenger thrust a small bundle towards her, saying, 'Take this.' When the stewardess realised that the bundle was in fact a used nappy, she declined the offer, telling the passenger that she needed to dispose of it herself in the toilet. But the passenger didn't want to move, and thrust it more forcefully at the stewardess, who explained that as she was serving food it would be unhygienic to handle a used nappy. This was too much for the furious passenger, who flung the nappy full force at the stewardess. It opened mid-flight, sending heavy chunks of baby faeces around the area. The two women then started to fight on the floor, and had to be separated by passengers.

On a Paris–Toronto flight in September 2000, cabin crew noticed a woman in her mid-forties taking surreptitious swigs of a bottle of cognac. Well used to passengers with fear of flying seeking to calm themselves down by any means at their disposal, they thought little of it until she started yelling at her fellow passengers about halfway through the flight. Alarmed, they asked her to keep quiet, but she responded badly to the request, getting up from her seat and hitting a flight attendant on the arm. She then returned to her seat and started to attack a neighbouring male passenger. Flight staff again attempted to calm her down, whereupon she started to throw newspapers and magazines around the cabin, then got down on all fours and crawled up and down the aisle, growling like a dog and biting flight attendants.

After she had hit another flight attendant in the face, bitten the finger of a male steward and tried to throttle another member of the cabin crew, she was tied to her chair by the arms and legs, although they could not prevent her from continuing to snarl. On arrival in Toronto she was arrested.

Carry-on storage space varies widely from plane to plane, and the lack of available space is a common complaint among frequent flyers. One passenger, among the last to board a plane, lost his rag when he found that there was no room in the overhead bin above his seat. Rather than search for a bin where there was room, he started to take the bags out of the bin and throw them on to the floor, replacing them with his own. Responding to cries from angry passengers, a female flight attendant returning to work after a double mastectomy and multiple sclerosis heard from them what had happened.

When she told the bag-flinging passenger that he couldn't do that, he broke her jaw with one punch.

For some people in-flight movies don't provide quite enough entertainment for the duration of the flight. On one flight from New York to Los Angeles, a man started to throw peanuts at another passenger sitting across the aisle. When the first one landed, the victim ignored it, assuming it to be the work of a bored child, or simply an accident. When the second landed, he knew it was no accident, and looked up to see who had thrown the salted nut. It wasn't hard to work out, and he glared at the offender, sure that he would now be too embarrassed to carry on. But a third landed soon after, bouncing off his eye, and he warned the nut-tosser not to do it again, or he'd punch him. The threat fell on deaf ears, and after yet another peanut struck the man in the face, he rose, furious, and punched the tosser so hard that many passengers heard the man's jaw break even through their headphones. The plane was diverted to land at the nearest airport, and the nut-thrower ejected.

When a passenger in an aisle seat on a British Airways flight from London to Johannesburg took out his laptop, his neighbours probably assumed that he was going to catch up on his work; when he put headphones on they may have thought he was going to watch a film of his choice, none of the in-flight entertainment suiting his tastes. But when he loaded a hardcore porn film onto his laptop, grunts and groans leaking from his headphones, some of his fellow passengers thought he'd taken personal choice too far, and called for a steward. After the steward's request for the passenger to stop watching 'Anal Debutantes 3' in full view of other passengers was ignored, the captain was called upon to make the same request with more authority. But this time, as the captain threatened to pull the plug, the aroused passenger flew into a rage and had to be restrained by staff. He eventually received a three-year jail sentence from a British court.

On a Delta Airlines flight from London to New York a British passenger who had drunk six or seven beers before boarding continued to drink in first class until flight attendants refused to serve him any more, pointing out that he had become loud and abusive. Sadly such treatment only made him louder and more abusive, and his mood swung violently between rage and lewdness. He touched two of the female flight attendants in a sexually suggestive way, then threw salad over a neighbouring passenger and punched a flight attendant who attempted to restrain him. In the ensuing melee the passenger's lip was cut, and he drooled blood on the flight attendant who restrained him on the floor until the plane was diverted to Maine's Bangor airport.

December 1997. While flying from Baltimore to Los Angeles, a well-built college American football player returning from holiday began to wander up and down the aisles blessing the other passengers and proclaiming that he was Jesus Christ. 'Touch me and you'll live forever,' he told passengers. 'We're all going to go to heaven.' Some passengers were irritated, others scared, and a flight attendant who had worked previously as a psychiatric nurse became convinced that the passenger was suffering from a psychotic episode.

Trained in dealing with such incidents, she led the passenger towards the rear galley, away from the other passengers, whose complaints were becoming louder and more vociferous. She avoided attempting to manhandle him or rebuke him, but just spoke to him in a soothing tone until he closed his eyes, knelt on the carpet and began to pray. But as soon as the attendant relaxed he grabbed her breast.

He apologised, but then told her that he needed to bless the pilots – that he had a message he needed to deliver to them – and headed up the aisle towards the cockpit, deaf to the flight attendant's pleas. She called the cockpit crew and warned them to prepare themselves, and another member of the cabin crew blocked the entrance to the cockpit with a drinks trolley. The deranged passenger had by now arrived at the cockpit door and demanded to be let in. When the flight attendant refused to let him through, he was thrown to the floor.

The former psychiatric nurse now managed to calm the passenger down, and began again to lead him to the rear of the plane. But he suddenly became enraged, and threw her across three rows of seats, leaving her with extensive injuries. A US Marine and two off-duty pilots wrestled the passenger to the ground with the help of another passenger, and he was restrained with handcuffs and seatbelt extensions, although it took being sat on by the two off-duty pilots to stop him from thrashing around and biting his captors.

When the flight landed the female flight attendant was rushed to hospital, while the jock messiah was arrested and taken into custody. He admitted having taken LSD before the flight, and faced charges of aggravated assault and inter-ference with a flight crew.

October 1998. When Steve Handy, a drunk British passenger, was asked to stop smoking by a flight attendant, he hit her on the head with a large vodka bottle, leaving her with a wound requiring eighteen stitches.

January 1999. Another drunk Briton, halfway through a fourteen-hour flight, harassed the woman sitting next to him, ripping off then biting through her headphones, then punched the door window, breaking through the inner layer and threatening to cause a decompression. It took four flight attendants and four passengers to restrain him.

On 10 May 2001 a 28-year-old passenger on a KLM flight from Amsterdam to Newark was so incensed when members of the flight crew asked him to turn off his mobile phone that he spat on a flight attendant, then ripped up his passport and began to wave around a cane, threatening to hit crew and other passengers. He then moved seats to business class, telling crew members that he suffered from claustrophobia.

At 37,000 feet it occurred to him that it was a good idea to open the emergency exit, but fortunately due to cabin pressure this proved impossible. The passenger, described by a KLM spokesman as 'clearly unstable', was then handcuffed by the captain and guarded by two passengers until the plane landed in the USA, whereupon he was flown back to the Netherlands under secure care.

On a flight from Miami to San Juan, Puerto Rico, a passenger walked to the back of the plane then ran down the aisle, slapping passengers' heads as he went. When a pregnant flight attendant attempted to remonstrate with him, he kicked her to the ground, then bit a young boy on the arm. At this, crew members restrained and handcuffed him, and he was arrested on arrival.

On a September 2003 United Airlines flight from Hawaii to Los Angeles a pious holidaymaker had to be restrained after he annoyed fellow passengers by quoting loudly from the Bible while walking up and down the aisle. Passengers held him down while an air steward duct-taped the impromptu preacher to his chair, finally silencing him with a strip of tape across the mouth.

On a July 1997 flight from Houston, Texas, a couple became agitated after being denied an upgrade to first class from their coach-class seats. When they were told to return to their seats the man grabbed two coffee pots and scalded a pair of flight attendants with the boiling liquid, then attempted to open the forward aircraft door, while telling his partner to enter the cockpit. She kicked the cockpit door until a blowout panel shattered, but an off-duty pilot in the cockpit kept the door closed. Cabin crew and passengers struggled to restrain the incensed couple until the plane was landed and the couple taken into custody.

In August 2002 a British man in his fifties was flying to Florida from Manchester to surprise his relatives at his son's wedding at the Cypress Gardens theme park, although he had not been invited. The passenger had been drinking heavily on the flight, and attendants had twice confiscated bottles of Jameson's whiskey from him before he embarked on the series of incidents that led to him being restrained and then arrested. He tried to open the plane's door in mid-flight, verbally abused a boy sitting next to him, threatened to kill a fellow passenger, slammed a flight attendant against a bathroom door and had to be restrained several times by other passengers.

An August 2002 Air France flight from Paris to Oslo was forced to make an emergency landing in Belgium after a 31-year-old passenger stripped naked and tried to force his way into the cockpit. He was arrested on landing and later released without charge; authorities were uncertain as to why he'd stripped and tried to storm the cockpit.

A JMC flight from Newcastle to Tenerife was forced to divert and land in Portugal after a female care worker became drunk, threatening and abusive. She had been drinking a rum and blackcurrant cordial mixture, and shortly after takeoff started to shout and swear at her boyfriend then kick the back of the seat in front of her. A court later heard that she had been drinking heavily to combat her fear of flying.

A Vietnamese tourist on a flight to Las Vegas got up from his seat and demanded a drink from flight attendants, but was told to wait his turn. Incensed, he overturned the drinks tray, spilling scalding coffee on a woman and her baby, and assaulted several other passengers on his way back to his seat, leaving a twelve-year-old girl with bruises. He was arrested on arrival in Las Vegas.

On a British Airways flight from Boston to London, an American passenger became enraged when he learned that the plane was due to land at Heathrow rather than Gatwick Airport. He attacked flight attendants, injuring one, and then, while being escorted off the plane by police, he grabbed an officer's gun and tried to shoot his escort then himself; the gun failed to go off.

A trip to China for a group of Russian tourists in the summer of 2003 ended badly when a number of them had to go to hospital immediately on returning to Vladivostok airport. They had got extremely drunk during the flight, and had started to argue; and the argument had then turned into a fight. In the affray at least two passengers – a 31-year-old man and a 33-year-old woman – were bitten, and one man suffered from concussion. The group was reported to have continued to fight even when they arrived at Vladivostok bus station.

I saw a fight break out on a holiday plane to Mallorca once. I was sitting across the aisle and behind a bit from a few lads who were getting stuck in to the bevvies as soon as the plane took off. Actually they were probably getting stuck in before, even though it was an 8 a.m. takeoff. Anyway, complimentary drinks had been brought round, and obviously all these boys had lager to add to the ones they'd taken on board. You could see the stewardess's fixed smile waver slightly as she dealt with these types, but they seemed to be in a good mood, and they weren't singing yet, so she left them to it.

The trouble started when one of them, the one nearest the aisle, took off his shoes and socks and put his feet on the meal tray, then started paring his toenails with a pair of clippers. The one sitting next to him whispered something to him, and all three of them started giggling. Then the one doing his toenails started to angle his foot, and aim it. After a couple of failed attempts, he must have managed to get a bit of nail to hit one of the people across the aisle and one row ahead from them. In fact I don't think it just hit this woman, but actually went into her drink.

Anyway, she went ballistic. I think she may have had a few herself, but she sat up, looked round, said something to the person sitting next to her then turned around and saw these boys giggling. The one who'd done it had taken his foot down now, but she was in no doubt that it had been them, and got up to give them a piece of her mind. She really laid into the one at the end of the aisle – at least she picked the right one! – pulling his hair and slapping him, until a steward came over and calmed her down. By this time the other two lads were in tears from laughing so hard. I don't know what happened after the flight, but I don't think it was taken any further. (HN, Norwich)

Two men were fined $480 each in separate incidents a few days apart in July 1999 for urinating on passengers and airplane seats during flights to Amsterdam. In the first incident a Norwegian man drank copious quantities of whisky and vodka while waiting 26 hours in Cairo for a flight to Amsterdam; 'Once airborne, the man felt the urge to relieve himself and dampened the three nearest seats,' a military police spokesman was quoted as saying.

On 29 July an American passenger drank eight cans of beer while en route to Amsterdam then took down his trousers, stumbled down the aisle with a beer in his hand and finally urinated over three seats and his neighbour's sleeve. He was duly overpowered by flight attendants who pulled up his trousers and alerted the Amsterdam authorities. The airline pressed charges against the American passenger for cleaning costs and causing distress to fellow passengers with his 'shocking behaviour'.

Flight attendants are often at the sharp end of complaints from passengers, not only in-flight but also on the ground. When the Dallas/Fort Worth airport had been closed due to bad weather for several hours, tensions were running high among the disgruntled passengers, whose planes had been prevented from leaving. One young female prospective passenger walked up to a female flight attendant and told her, 'I'm sorry, but I have to do this.' She then punched the attendant full in the face, breaking her nose.

In another similar incident at Newark International Airport in July 1999, a 50-year-old Continental Airlines gate agent was pushed violently to the floor after telling a passenger to wait at the boarding gate. He suffered fractures to his neck and spine.

Not all alcohol abuse ends in violence, but other outcomes can be equally unsavoury, as the following account makes clear:

Our flight from Newark back to London had been delayed for a few hours, but we'd already checked in and there wasn't much food available. But there was a bar, and a lot of the passengers propped it up, probably trying to kid themselves that eating peanuts while drinking Bloody Marys constituted some kind of meal. When we finally took off, the plane turned out to be about a third empty, and a few people asked for seconds of the food, which was pretty standard airplane lasagne. There were a couple of real lardbucket characters flying as well, and I was sitting a few rows back from them;

not wanting to be nosy, but I could see they were trying the patience of the stewardesses by asking for seconds and then, impossibly, thirds. That was probably why they didn't respond when one of the passengers pressed the call button – they probably thought he wanted more food. Actually it was more likely that what he wanted was a sick bag, as the plane's turnaround must have been too fast for them to have restocked; his neighbour and fellow porker didn't seem to have one either. Before anyone could get to him and see what he wanted, he'd tried to get up and in the process sprayed three helpings of lasagne down his front and into the aisle. The sight – or maybe just the smell – of copious quantities of what must have been regurgitated red wine mixed with partly digested meat and pasta sent his friend off as well, and this was enough to have its impact on everyone. As the cabin crew looked on in horror one passenger after another scrabbled frantically in the pouch in the seat in front of them then sprayed warm lasagne on the floor, until the aisle was running with a rich stinking mess. A few passengers tried to get up and make it to the toilet, but there are never enough for a situation like this, and some had the added ignominy of feeling the contents of their stomachs forcing themselves through their noses. I think even a couple of the stewards might have succumbed as well. As for me, maybe I did, maybe I didn't . . . (JS, Oxford)

And some passengers suffer from an unexpected form of exposure:

On a holiday flight back from the Caribbean I saw a short, big-bottomed old woman leave the toilet and head back to her seat. Either she was too tired to realise, or she'd had a few too many drinks, whatever, but she'd forgotten to pull her knickers and joggers up, and they were hanging around her knees. Most of the passengers who'd noticed just turned away and tried to look at something else – it wasn't something you really wanted to look at – until a stewardess noticed and pulled her back towards the toilet. Not a moment too soon . . . (DI, Cheltenham)

The following legal affidavit is quoted at length for the incongruous relationship between the dry legal descriptions and the outrageous behaviour described. This is one of the most notorious instances of air rage ever: the 'turd on a tray' incident. In order to protect the guilty, the defendant's name has here been shortened to F:

The defendant, F, had been a passenger on United Airlines Flight 976 from Buenos Aires to JFK International Airport. Prior to the flight taking off, F began to drink alcoholic beverages and continued to drink during the course of the flight. Initially, these beverages were served by members of the flight crew, as required by flight regulations. However, F eventually started getting up and serving himself.

At this point, F was told by members of the flight crew that it was against regulations for him to serve himself alcohol. F ignored them and continued to serve himself. Flight crew members then advised F that he would not be permitted to drink any more alcoholic beverages. In response to this, F began to demand that they serve him more. He then approached a male flight attendant and demanded that the flight attendant give him more drink. When the attendant refused, F threatened him, indicating that he was going to 'bust his ass'.

At this point, another male flight attendant received notification that a passenger in the plane (not F) felt ill. This flight attendant went to the cockpit and retrieved a first-aid kit. While he was walking back towards the ill passenger, he was confronted by F. F harassed the flight attendant, demanding that he provide F with more alcohol. According to the flight attendant, this confrontation with F prevented the flight attendant from assisting the ill passenger in a timely manner.

At one point in the flight, F approached a female flight attendant and demanded that she provide him with more alcoholic beverages. When she refused, F pushed her by placing both hands on her chest, causing her to fall into one of the seats.

A male flight attendant then entered the first-class section and saw F with his pants and underwear down defaecating on a service cart used by the flight crew. F then used linen napkins as toilet paper and wiped his hands on various service counters and service implements used by the crew. F also tracked faeces throughout the aircraft.

The Captain of the aircraft was notified of F's behaviour. In response, the Captain suspended all food and beverage service on the flight due to the possibility of an infectious condition. At this time, the flight was approximately four hours from New York. In addition, the Captain suspended the FAA required rest periods for the flight crew so that they could continue to attend to F.

Mile High

It happens for all kinds of reasons. Maybe they've watched too many of those bear-rug sex scenes in 70s *Airport* movies, and can't get the association out of their mind; maybe they've indulged a bit too much in the duty-free spirits and can't restrain themselves; maybe they've heard about it and want to see what it's like; and maybe they're just bored. Whatever the case, a survey carried out by online travel company Opodo revealed that nearly ten per cent of air travellers claimed to have joined the mile-high club, with more than half the rest hoping to join in the future.

Some prefer to do it in the seats, perhaps with the decency of a rug thrown over their writhing bodies; others prefer the privacy of a toilet, although the accidental pressing of the call button – again and again and again – can get a little tiring for staff, and more portly pleasure-seekers have been known to get stuck.

Airlines vary in their attitude towards sky sex – most treat it as an offence, but Virgin Atlantic once ran an ad campaign featuring Mike Myers as Austin Powers, straddling the fuselage of a jumbo jet and proclaiming, 'Virgin Shagatlantic

– yeah, baby.' Virgin boss Richard Branson clarified the airline's position by stating that 'We're not the type of airline that bangs on bathroom doors.'

For some companies, particularly in the US, the chance to join the mile-high club is their sole offering. But one such flight came to the wrong kind of sticky end when a couple attempted to hijack the plane, which was flying over Key West, Florida, and have it flown to Cuba; after a struggle with the pilot, one of the hijackers fell on the throttle, causing the plane to crash into the sea.

The following stories describe some of the more notorious incidents of sex in the sky:

During a flight from London to Vancouver in 1992, passengers were nonplussed while a couple had sex under a blanket, many barely batting an eyelid as they flicked through their in-flight magazines or stared glumly at the romantic comedy being played out on their miniature TV screens; crew members were similarly uninterested, having more pressing needs such as trying to calm squalling children and flirting with the flight crew. But as soon as the couple had finished, each sparked up a cigarette, and crew and other passengers went ballistic in their efforts to stop them.

In 1998, on a South African Airways flight from London to Durban, a couple undressed from the waist down, pushed their seats back into the rest position and began to have full sex in view of other passengers. Passengers called for crew members to disengage the couple, but their best efforts were not enough. After a quarter of an hour, during which the pilot had made several pleas for them to stop over the intercom, he finally left the cockpit to manually force them apart, yelling at them, 'This is not a shag house!' They were later charged with violating airline guidelines.

On a transatlantic American Airlines flight from Dallas to Manchester in 1999, two strangers, both married to someone else, got drunk on wine, port and cognac, and started to get cosy under a blanket when the lights were dimmed for the in-flight movie. But soon the blanket and most of their clothes were off, and efforts by cabin crew to stop their lewd display, or at least to encourage them to be more discreet, were unsuccessful. One airline source was quoted as saying that 'Nothing and no one, short of a bucket of cold water, could have stopped them. They were determined to continue until their passions were spent . . . and they did.'

The pair was arrested when they arrived at Manchester Airport, and were later fined for being drunk on board a plane; passing sentence, the judge maintained that they had already suffered substantially from the publicity surrounding the case.

On a BA flight from Nairobi, a couple got stuck having sex in the gap behind the last row of seats, and had to call cabin crew to help free them. During another flight, on an Air

France plane travelling from Nice to London, passengers called out 'Vive le sport!' when a couple left the toilet. The young woman, who emerged behind her boyfriend, had forgotten to put her boob tube back on.

12. WHERE THE WILD THINGS ARE

'There can be no covenant between lions and men'
Homer, *Iliad XXII*

The lure of exotic animals draws tourists all around the world, from the vast game reserves of sub-Saharan Africa to the Amazonian rainforest. Yet many tourists, expecting nature to be the consumable commodity they see on TV, react in shock and disbelief as they lose digits, limbs and even lives to the enraged beasts they have travelled so far to see. Suckered by the cynical lies peddled by soft-toy manufacturers, they have forgotten what the word 'wild' means when applied to animals, and learn all too late that their bite is indeed often worse than their bark. Zoo diets are routinely spiced up with an impromptu arm, and in safari parks the world over lions wait with slavering jaws for the tourist who has to go the extra step for the perfect photo.

Nature Red in Tooth and Claw

Most people are well aware that they need to keep large carnivorous animals at a safe distance, but it's not only these kinds of animals that have attacked tourists. One eleven-year-old visitor to New Orleans Zoo in 1939 tried to feed a zebra, safe in the knowledge that it was a placid herbivore. But the animal, its instincts perverted by life in confinement, tore off the child's middle finger for a snack.

In 1952 a 32-year-old visitor to Tarong Park Zoo in Sydney, Australia, wanted to get a closer look at the cassowaries. These small flightless birds, related to the ostrich, are under four feet tall, and so the visitor had few qualms about jumping the fence. But as soon as he was in the cage they attacked him, knocking him to the ground and pecking and slashing at his body. He eventually escaped, but only with around thirty slash and puncture wounds and a collapsed lung.

In a more recent incident in 1993, a father and son visited the Moffitt Ranch, a game reserve near San Antonio, on holiday. When they passed a nilgai, a large species of antelope, they stopped the car to pet the ruminant. At first the animal remained docile and allowed itself to be petted; but then, as though to remind father and son of the park's rules regarding petting animals, it tore open the father's leg with one slash of its curved horns, severing the femoral artery. The father bled to death, as the antelope watched and the panicked son cried for help.

It's not only horns and teeth that can injure tourists. One visitor to Yellowstone Park, California, in July 1999, was attacked by a bison. He was about fifteen yards from the resting animal when it suddenly stood up and appeared to charge towards him. The tourist dived to the ground and decided to play dead, whereupon the bison sat on him. He suffered from multiple rib fractures and was taken to a local hospital.

Never Get Out of the Car

Another drive-through safari park incident involved more dangerous animals, the titular carnivores of Irvine's Lion Country Safari Park. Ideally such reserves give more freedom to visitor and animal, allowing both to roam around without the ignominy of being restricted to cages or concrete walkways. But visitors don't always put safety first. One elderly woman was so excited to see a lion bounding towards her that she stopped her car and rolled the window down rather than up. 'Tiny', as the cat had been affectionately dubbed, managed to scalp the unwary visitor before being driven off.

In another incident in Safari Park, a wild game reserve in Alicante, Spain, two German tourists ignored signs posted throughout the park in a variety of languages, including German, warning them not to open the windows and to remain inside their cars at all times. For reasons unknown, the Germans not only got out of their car but locked it behind them, whereupon they were attacked by three Bengal tigers, which quickly silenced their screams by breaking their necks. When security guards arrived on-scene they found the man gutted and the woman beheaded.

And if safari parks in Western countries can turn holiday to nightmare for visitors who refuse to obey the rules, how much worse the situations careless tourists can fall into in Africa's national parks and game reserves. Many fatalities have been incurred by tourists leaving the safety of their cars or tour buses simply to get a better photo. In Ruaha National Park, Tanzania, in January 2001, a safari tourist met with a grisly end when she stepped out of the tour bus to frame the perfect safari picture, being trampled to death along with her camera by an enraged elephant.

In Kruger National Park, South Africa, a tourist decided to ignore the explicit warnings from park authorities to stay inside her car when she spotted a lioness and her cubs. According to her husband, who stayed inside the car, she stated that the cubs were not posed properly for her photo, and then stepped out to rearrange them, picking one up so that it was closer to the others. The lioness pounced and shared the visitor with her cubs.

In the Hwange National Park, Zimbabwe, a Japanese tourist got out of his jeep to get a better picture of a male lion eating his prey, and was torn limb from limb and eaten himself for his pains. His brother wisely stayed in the jeep and filmed the grisly incident, then tried to sell the video to local news teams.

An Australian state minister was reported to be considering new laws to protect 'people too stupid to protect themselves', after watching a video of tourists patting Great White sharks on the head. The sharks were filmed feeding on a whale carcass off the coast near Adelaide; tourists were filmed stroking the heads of the sharks and climbing on top of the carcass while it was being eaten, to pose for souvenir photographs. As one hand reaches out to tickle a Great White, a voice can be heard exclaiming, 'Harry, are you an idiot or what?'

Bad as Binky

Drunk or sober, many tourists fall victim to cutesy renditions of savage animals and forget that zoo cages are there for a very good reason. Polar bears are a salutary case in point, being some of the most ill-tempered and vicious animals on the planet and characteristically indulging in behaviour entirely at odds with the cuddly bear images promoted by certain confectionery manufacturers.

In Alaska Zoo, Anchorage, the polar bear known as Binky – the name giving no indication of the power of his arm or sharpness of his claws – was involved in several such incidents. In the first, two drunk teenage visitors to the zoo decided to swim with polar bears, and climbed over two fences to get to the pool. There, Binky took offence and mauled the first intruder, leaving him with severe prostate damage; the second teenager escaped unscathed. Ironically enough, at the time of the attack a new enclosure was being built, as the existing enclosure was considered to be too elaborate for its purpose of keeping the polar bears inside.

A few years later a 29-year-old Australian tourist spotted

Binky sleeping inside the enclosure. Enthralled, and coming from a country that lacks bears of any description, she scaled two fences, secure in the knowledge that the cage bars themselves would keep her from Binky's grip. Sadly she snagged her shorts on the second fence, and her struggle awoke Binky, who reached out between the bars and pulled the tourist off the fence and towards the bars for a slow mauling. Fortunately she was saved by his fascination with her feet; while he chewed on one of her trainers she managed to extricate her foot and pull herself to safety. Binky kept the trainer to the end of his days, and the local fire department later printed T-shirts bearing the slogan 'Bad as Binky', with a drawing of Binky chewing on a trainer.

The tourist, talking to press while she was in hospital being treated for a broken leg and gashes to her leg and body, complained of the lack of warning signs, stating that 'it didn't occur to me that it was vicious'. She did, however, admit that 'it was the dumbest thing I've ever done in my life', and put the incident in perspective by pointing out that, 'It was like King Kong, you know?'

It's not only polar bears that have caused problems for tourists. In January 2003 a British tourist visiting a zoo in Benimantell, near Alicante, Spain, strayed from her tour group and tried to stroke a caged lion. A lioness called Marta pounced on her hand and eventually ripped her arm off at the elbow. Other lions then joined in, and a tussle ensued for possession of the severed limb.

A bad-tempered sea-lion received a permanent police patrol after biting tourists in Caleta Coloso, Chile. In September 2002 police assigned an extra patrol to the area after the sea-lion, an old male known as 'Grandpa', had bitten eighteen tourists so far that year. Police said that they were ramping up their presence due to concerns that 'this one grumpy sea-lion will try and bite everyone', and pointed out that although they had put up signs warning people not to approach or feed the sea-lions, 'there's always a few people who have too much to drink on holiday and try to pet them.'

A bite from a 200-kilo sea-lion is a serious injury: one tourist had to have 100 stitches in his leg after arousing Grandpa's wrath.

Pets' Corner

Not all animal-related incidents involving tourists end in attack. Some tourists keep animals as pets, and travel with them in what might be considered inappropriate situations, such as taking them on planes. Unless an animal is a 'celebrity pet' – an animal that features in adverts or films, for instance – most airlines will insist that it rides in the hold. Some tourists, loath for their furry, feathered or scaled friend to suffer such indignities, will try to smuggle their pet on board, and pet rats, snakes and spiders have all caused problems mid-flight.

At Glasgow airport in July 2000 customs officials stopped and searched a tourist, only to find that her 'snakeskin' belt was alive. She had worn the python tied around her waist in an ingenious bid to fool customs into thinking it was an item of clothing; in fact she was trying to smuggle it in from the USA. Customs in Europe and the USA routinely confiscate items made from crocodile leather, ivory or other proscribed materials, or parts of endangered animals destined for speciality restaurants and practitioners of folk medicine, but to seize live animals is rare.

In another incident in October 2003 a Swedish tourist was arrested in Australia after flying from Bangkok with eight baby snakes in his trousers. The Swede had hoped to fund an eight-day holiday in Australia by selling the snakes, four venomous baby king cobras and four baby emerald tree boas, which were strapped to his legs in home-made pouches.

In April 2002 an Italian tourist who was travelling around Europe with his chicken was arrested in the Netherlands after having been seen taking his pet for a walk. At the police station the chicken was seized and summarily executed. The tourist owner was released without charge, but he had to pay for the services of the vet who killed his pet and an animal ambulance. The country was suffering from an outbreak of bird flu, with a corresponding ban on the transportation of poultry, of which the tourist claimed to know nothing. He was unsurprisingly disappointed by the development, and left the police station vowing to file a complaint at the Italian consulate.

In October 2002 a tourist was charged with stealing an alligator from a Florida golf course. Witnesses alleged that they had seen the tourist make a noose with a line designed for feeding live alligators, and use it to capture a three-foot alligator wandering around the golf course. According to a local newspaper the tourist was found in his hotel parking lot holding the alligator to his body, with one hand around its mouth to keep it from calling out. He was charged with alligator poaching and petty theft and taken to a local jail.

It's not the first time tourists have fallen foul of the law for mishandling alligators. In 2001 two tourists were arrested after having snatched an alligator from the same golf course and taking it to their hotel pool, where they were found by police watching it swim.

Most tourists travel with some kind of budget, but some will stop at nothing to cut costs. In April 2002 a tourist from Ireland became the first person to eat a live cockroach to get free entry into a New Zealand tourist attraction. Saving just over £6, he told journalists that 'I felt a bit sick afterwards, like I'd just eaten something bad', but reassured them that it wasn't as bad as eating sprouts as a child. Asked to describe the taste, he compared it to chewing a twig, then added, 'There wasn't a lot of taste to it to be honest but that might have been the excitement of the moment, but it was definitely worth it – plus we got our $20 (NZ) back.'

Two Apocryphal Stories

Two Scousers have become rich from promoting successful clubs in the Liverpool area. Fancying themselves as a cut above the hoi polloi, they now shun holiday activities such as sunning themselves in Ibiza or the Costa del Sol and decide to pursue more gentrified activities, such as shooting grouse on a country manor farm.

They go out with their shotguns, but find it difficult to shoot anything, and return to the farm frustrated. The owner of the farm sees that they have had no success, and says to one of them, 'While you have the guns, I've got a lame horse that needs shooting. Normally I'd have to pay to have it put down, but as you're here you might as well shoot it for me.'

The Scouser thinks, 'Great! I won't tell my friend, but I'll just go out and shoot the horse.' So he rejoins his friend in the field, having been shown by the farmer which horse to shoot, and while listening to his friend moan about the difficulty of shooting anything, says, 'Watch this.' He then raises his shotgun and shoots the lame horse in the head.

His friend says, 'Brilliant!' and raises his shotgun in turn, to blast a large hole in the side of the farmer's prize cow. (MB, London)

There's a few places in Cambodia where you can go and hire guns to shoot: handguns are pretty cheap, machine guns a bit more expensive, and some people blow a whole load of cash on using rocket launchers. They don't really have much you can shoot at, though, and some people get imaginative about what they're going to use for target practice. When I was at one of these places a guy from London rocked up with two chickens and a handgun, but he didn't tie their feet down or anything, and totally missed them. Not sure if he managed to catch them after that again – they probably ended up in some Cambodian family's soup that night.

There was a story going around as well about two Australians, two rocket launchers and a cow. Now a cow's a bit more expensive than a chicken, but it's also a much easier target to hit and will make a much more impressive explosion than a chicken. Apparently the Aussies had egged each other on to do it – they were both pissed, naturally – and they'd gone around first trying to buy a cow. Most of the locals were totally bewildered by what they'd want a cow for, but they had enough money, and managed to track one down pretty easily. Then they took it to the firing range and again showed enough money to get a couple of rocket launchers, no questions asked, and blow it sky high. I don't think you really need two rocket launchers to blow a cow up, but they probably just couldn't agree between themselves which one was going to get to shoot the cow. Bet the Cambodians would rather they'd just shot a bullet into its head, rather than ruin all that good meat, but they probably still got the legs. (NT, Coventry)

13. WHEN DISASTER STRIKES

Always travel with insurance, we are told. But no cover, no matter how comprehensive, can insure the bungling holiday-maker against their own stupidity, nor against being singled out by the capricious hand of fate for a grotesque and demeaning encounter with pain. Accidents will happen, we are told. Well, yes, but couldn't some of the following have been avoided?

Cape Town, South Africa, September 2002: a 21-year-old Welsh engineering student was on a bus returning with friends from a trip to the wineland town of Stellenbosch when he decided to moon passing motorists by baring his buttocks at the back window of the bus. Unfortunately for him the window was an emergency exit and gave way, sending the half-naked man falling into the middle lane of the busy road. Traffic was brought to a standstill as paramedics treated the man, who was later hospitalised for severe abrasions and loss of blood.

The Grand Canyon in Arizona has a fence going around the more dangerous stretches, to stop unsteady tourists falling off. Some of these overlooks have small towering plateaus a small distance away, and tourists use them as wishing wells, tossing coins onto the tops. One keen tourist climbed over the fence to jump onto one of these, and filled a bag with loose change. But when he tried to jump back, his heavy bag pulled him back and several tourists were treated to a view of him plummeting to the bottom of the Canyon.

On an SAS Boeing 767 flying from Oslo, Norway, to New York, an American tourist decided to flush the toilet she'd just used while still sitting on it. Sadly the act created such strong suction that she was held fast to the bowl. When cabin crew heard her pitiful cries for help they tried to lever her off but were unable to move her. She was then obliged to spend the rest of the flight – around five hours or so – stuck in the toilet. The airline which provided the flight declared that she was to receive compensation for her embarrassment and lack of comfort.

In August 2000 a tourist sued Disney World after a coffee spillage caused him to have 'pigmentation changes to his genitals'. The jury awarded him $668,000.

On holiday in the summer of 2002 in Italy, a 53-year-old Glaswegian man decided to show off for the benefit of onlookers at the top of a mountain. With a cry of 'Hey – watch this!' he attached a climber's snap hook to an unused overhead tram cable and launched himself off the top of the mountain in a daring attempt to ride all the way down to the bottom. He clearly hadn't reckoned on the force of gravity and the steepness of the mountain, however, as he accelerated uncontrollably and crashed into rocks after only a few seconds, before bouncing for 200 metres down the slope and crashing into a pylon. He did not survive the incident.

A hapless American tourist's October 2003 visit to Bavaria finished with a crunch when his car's automatic navigation system led him to drive through a supermarket's doors and crash into a row of shelves. The man, who had been celebrating his sixty-eighth birthday that day, told local police that he had been relying on the automatic navigation system as he was unfamiliar with the area, and that he had not noticed the supermarket's doors until he had crashed through them. He was told he would have to pay for the damage caused.

During a traditional Maori welcome to New Zealand in the summer of 2003, an English tourist had his jaw broken by a traditional Maori fighting weapon. The Maori challenger involved had stepped forwards to avoid hitting people behind him with his metre-long wooden taiaha, which was described as swinging 'over his head like a helicopter', and accidentally clubbed the Englishman's face instead. The holidaymaker required surgery and was taken to hospital with loose teeth, deep facial cuts and a broken jaw. Organisers of the welcome ceremony have advised taiaha performers to keep well back of spectators in future.

14. THE WORLD'S WORST TOURISTS

Who are the worst tourists in the world? Well, the rude ones, obviously. But in a bid to spark off a fresh round of national stereotyping, Microsoft's online travel service Expedia ran a survey in the summer of 2003 in which tourist offices from seventeen popular destinations worldwide were asked to vote on their least favourite tourists. The ranking, from best to worst, is as follows:

Germans +41
Americans +32
Japanese +24
Italians +10
French +5
Norwegians +5
Swedish +5
Spanish +4
Canadians +4
Chinese +3
Thais +3

Dutch +3

Brazilians −1

Danes −1

Polish −1

Russians −2

Argentinians −3

New Zealanders −3

Czechs −3

Finnish −3

Indians −4

Irish −6

Israelis −6

British −44

The tourist offices awarded points to each country according to criteria such as whether they behaved well, whether they tipped well, what efforts they made to understand another country's culture, etc. German tourists ranked highest for their behaviour and their attempts to speak the local language; Americans were the most polite and the best tippers, and the Italians were the most adventurous tourists. British tourists were the worst behaved, most rude, least likely to learn the language and least enthusiastic about eating local food, generally referred to as 'that foreign muck'.

The survey is probably flawed – what about the Germans and their sun loungers? – by the fact that the majority of tourist offices targeted to fill in the survey were located in places to which British tourists go on package holidays. This meant that the survey focused principally on British tourist trash – the pissed-up 'Ibiza lobster' rather than the country's sensitive, well-travelled 'polite Peruvian explorer'. There's also the matter of confirmation bias – people see what they expect to see, although the behaviour of individuals is so diverse that any stereotype can be used to fit any nationality and be confirmed. Groups tend moreover to bring out the worst behaviour in individuals, who will do things when egged on by friends that they'd never do by themselves.

Then again, national stereotypes – even (or perhaps especially) within the European Union – are deeply ingrained, for all the efforts of politicians and educators to eradicate them. After all, we all know that heaven is where the police are British, the lovers are French, the mechanics are German, the cooks are Italian and it's all organised by the Swiss; and hell is where the police are German, the mechanics are French, the cooks are British, the lovers are Swiss and it's all organised by the Italians.

Actually politicians aren't averse to a bit of name-calling themselves. An unseemly debate was sparked off during the summer of 2003 when Silvio Berlusconi, the Italian prime minister, told a German MEP that the German would be perfect for a film role as a commandant in a Nazi concentration camp, possibly thinking of such Italian movie classics as *Ilsa, She-Wolf of the SS* and *SS Experiment Camp*.

The furore that predictably ensued was only made worse when Stefano Stefani, Italy's minister for tourism, made the following comments in an open letter published in an Italian newspaper:

We know the Germans well – these stereotyped blondes with ultra-nationalist pride, indoctrinated for as long as we can remember to feel top of the class at any price.

And just like any self-respecting 'top of the class' pupils, they never miss an opportunity to behave in an arrogant manner. They rowdily invade our beaches ... I have never considered the Germans to be endowed with a particularly refined sense of humour.

Stefani went on to accuse German tourists of drinking too much, eating too many potatoes and indulging in burping contests. He tried to make amends after his uncharacteristic outburst by inviting German chancellor Gerhard Schröder to visit him on holiday, conceding that Schröder was 'not as bad as most Germans'. But the tourism minister was not long for his job, and resigned a week later, telling press 'I love Germany' during his resignation speech.

It wasn't enough. Germans began to boycott pasta and flood the Italian embassy in Berlin with faxes and letters of complaint. German women sunbathed topless on the Italian embassy lawn, presumably to combat the stereotype of German women all being overmuscled shotputters. Many Germans also cancelled their holidays to Italy, although Germany's most popular tabloid newspaper – *Bild Zeitung* – sent a planeload of beer-swilling readers to Rimini to drink, burp and eat as many potatoes as they could. The paper also published an ongoing daily list of useful phrases in Italian for prospective visitors, such as 'Keep your oily eyes off my wife.'

All this was good news for the Brits, of course, who are routinely considered the nuisance neighbours of Europe, as it distracted attention – however briefly – from their own grotesque holiday indiscretions. For about a week, anyway. During that week, journalists happily reminisced over stories such as the following, which came from the former editor of the *Today* programme, Rod Liddle, on Radio 4:

An Italian friend of his was working in Rimini as a lifeguard when a German couple came up to him and told him that their five-year-old child was missing. The lifeguard picked up the megaphone and addressed the crowds on the beach. 'A German child is missing,' he told the assembled sunbathers. 'And for every one German child that goes missing, there will be ten Italian children executed . . .'

Well, if it's good enough for politicians, it's good enough for us. The following section indulges in shameless stereotyping while providing a helpful guide to spotting which countries tourists come from, as well as providing strange but true country-specific stories that don't really fit anywhere else. Readers are reminded to treat all individuals as individuals and not to make any assumptions about people they encounter, even if it is those annoying gangs of French schoolchildren perpetually blocking London pavements.

USA

Loud Americans routinely shout across wide spaces – from one train platform to another, or across a big hall in a museum. One American newspaper article mentioned this in regard to security advice for Americans travelling abroad, telling readers to keep their voices down and learn to 'talk like a Canadian'.

They prefer to speak in English, usually reacting to a lack of understanding by repeating their sentence slowly and loudly, but will occasionally attempt Spanish, and often assume that this will also pass for French, Italian etc:

I always cringe when I hear Americans (or anyone) using Spanish in Italy because it's 'close enough'. I still laugh about this frustrated young woman trying to buy a train ticket using the following phrase: 'Voglio ain't yo quiero.' (GM, Austin)

On a tram in Vienna an American girl of around twenty walked up to a couple and asked them a question, in English. They smiled, and apologised, and said they did not speak English. She huffed away and hurried over to her friends, perplexed, and announced, quite loudly, 'They wouldn't answer me, they're speaking in some foreign language.' Argh. The runner-up is the little co-ed in Paris who screamed 'she just told me "non parlez anglais." How rude!' (TS, Washington)

We were having coffee and a snack in a small out-of-the-way cafe. I am fluent in Italian, and was trying to teach a friend some conversational phrases. Not too many people were in the cafe at the time and the owner (I presume) came over to us, obviously amused by his horrible pronunciation. He and I were talking when an American couple came in and asked the owner for directions (in English). The owner, who barely had any knowledge of English, shrugged his shoulders and shook his head and looked towards me. I was about to say something to the couple when the American man said in frustration (I guess he didn't have luck finding directions earlier), 'What the fuck! Don't any of these fucking idiots speak a word of fucking English? Jesus Christ! What is the matter with these people?'

Shocked at the horrible display of cultural ignorance and rudeness, I looked at the man and said, '*Guardare che cosa voi dicono, non conoscete mai chi può capirlo*!' The man looked at me with a questioning look. I looked him straight in the eye and translated, 'Watch what you say, you never know who can understand you.' He then looked at me and then his wife, grabbed her hand and stormed out. The owner smiled at me, kissed me on the cheek and later refused our money when we went to pay. (GM, Austin)

Clothes Both older and younger Americans wear shorts in inappropriate surroundings and on inappropriate body shapes, choosing their clothes to fit the calendar rather than the weather. Older Americans often dress in shell suits, while their younger countrymen prefer khakis, white T-shirts and baseball caps, with white socks and trainers. Everything has a logo – either GAP or the name of their college. Young American women abroad wear tight jeans over white trainers. Some Americans have taken to sewing Canadian flags on their backpacks to avoid stereotypes of the ugly American.

Physical attributes Men: strong jawlines, weak cheekbones. Many have square heads and thick necks, especially if they belong to a college fraternity. Women: big hair, perfect teeth, short, too much make-up. Americans of both sexes often walk with a very cocky, self-important swagger. They are also often extremely large – check out the following story:

I used to work at a car rental outlet at Heathrow, and we'd routinely rent cars to American tourists who wanted to drive around London for a day, then visit Windsor, Nottingham (for Sherwood Forest) and maybe some of the King Arthur stuff in Cornwall. I'd known some Americans were pretty fat, but I hadn't been to the States before, and so on one of my first days I was stunned to see this huge lard bucket of a man come to pick up a car. He wasn't even that tall, but must have weighed 25 stone or so. The car he'd hired wasn't that big, but it didn't occur to me that he might have problems using it, and I booked him in, gave him the keys and directed him to the car depot.

Normally car rental staff don't actually accompany customers to their cars – they're just given a bay number and have to find it by themselves – but this time the depot guard saw this guy coming round to pick up a car and thought it might break the monotony to help him. First thing the guy does when he gets to the car is to push the seat right back – probably standard practice for him, although his legs weren't that long, so there was only so far he could push it back before he wouldn't be able to drive the car at all. But that didn't end up being the problem this time. He sat in the seat and tried to pull the rest of his bulk in – one leg at a time, then grabbing at the folds of his stomach and pulling them across the steering wheel – but all he managed to do was jam himself in.

The guard had to look away to stop from giggling, but then had to help the guy when he realised he was actually stuck inside the car. Not only would he not be able to drive it – the steering wheel was wedged against his belly, hard – but he couldn't get out either. So the guard had to lean in and help the guy to rock himself back and forth, easing his way out of the car, until he'd managed to free himself. By this time he was sweating and furious, and all I knew about it at the time was him coming back to the office and demanding to know why he couldn't fit behind the wheel – didn't we have any American cars, etc.

With as straight a face as I could muster, I told him that he could change his booking and have a roomier car, but the poor guy was now so angry and embarrassed that he cancelled – losing some money in the process – and stormed off, presumably to find another car rental firm that specialised in oversized vehicles. (TI, Hounslow)

Behaviour Americans usually walk around in large groups, very slowly, especially in non-pedestrian areas, pointing at things in a none-too-subtle attempt to distract the attention of their companions while they read out factoids from their guidebooks relating to what they're pointing at. They always talk to the people they are with about what they are all doing together at that very moment, particularly regarding time and space, in some crazed imitation of a Peter and Jane book:

'We will be over there. We are going over there. Where will you be? Where is John? Is John with you? Oh, there you are, John. John is right behind you. Where will John be? John, we will be over there.'

This is followed by a re-narration of what they'd just said, to the people they'd just said it to, who'd experienced the same event: 'We were over there. We have been over there. Where were you? Was John with you? Oh, he was right there. John was right behind you. Where was John going? John, we were going over there.'

They are renowned for tipping heavily, even if the service is poor, and paradoxically assume everyone speaks English when they want to buy something or need information, but that nobody speaks English when they want to make rude comments about locals/other tourists.

The American attitude abroad is generally positive and optimistic, but can also be insensitive and dismissive of local culture – things are either 'kinda neat' or 'suck'. Everything is compared to America, with many tourists starting sentences 'In America ...' and ending them by pointing out how inferior other countries are. They are also notorious for wishing for things – usually American products – out loud. And I mean loud:

Visiting American rugby players were in a rather upscale Dublin bar, and kept demanding obscure American 'shots' like the purple hooter, as well as liquors like tequila and Jagermeister, which aren't commonly found in such places in Ireland. The bartender kept saying, 'How about a whiskey?' 'Maybe you'd like a Guinness?' and generally acting very courteous.

They kept complaining how no decent college bar [oxymoron] in the States would be without their novelty liquors. Finally the bartender – who had many other polite patrons to attend to – said, 'Then perhaps I can offer you the door?' and in one swift motion came out from behind the bar, took the most obstreporous of the bunch by the collar, and unceremoniously dumped him out.

When he returned, lightly wiping his hands with his Harp bartowel, he asked the lad's friends, 'And what can I get you gentlemen?' 'Guinness, please' was the almost universal reply of the former rowdies. (EN, Eureka)

My favourite ugly American incident occurred at a pub in Oxford where an eighteen-year-old guy from Houston was mad as all get-out that he couldn't get a BUD LIGHT like AT HOME. So he 'settled' for a Guinness (which is a luxury in the States). It was obvious after a bit of harassment that the bartender (an Oxford student) had had enough.

Finally this guy asked how late the pub was open. He couldn't believe it was only open until eleven when 'all the bars in Texas stay open until at least two.' The bartender was fed up. He put down the glass he was filling, leaned over the bar, and yelled to his dissatisfied customer, 'Well, you're not in Texas, are you? You're in England! So shut the fuck up and drink your beer!' It was so classic—I laughed all the way home. (EL, Newark)

Americans customarily wave large sums of money around in any public place – restaurants, hotel lobbies, crowded streets, the more people around the better. They then tell everyone where they are staying, along with information such as 'there's more where that came from' or 'I'm a millionaire.' If they are low on cash, flashing loads of jewellery usually works as a good alternative. They insist on paying for items using US dollars, and receiving change in said currency, or using credit cards in entirely unsuitable locations, e.g. developing world street markets. They are entirely unable to function with other currencies:

Imagine my horror in London when a group of Americans in front of us in a queue were trying to pay for their lunch and complaining (loudly) about the British coins, pounds and pence and so on, and yelling that they 'still don't understand all their complicated money' but added that 'inventing dollars and cents' was the best thing 'we' ever did for 'them'. It'd be different if it was funny, but everyone around just looked disgusted. (GM, London)

Eating Americans cut their food, put down their knife, swap their fork to their right hand and eat. American women ask many questions about the food they're about to order/eat: 'Is there egg in this pasta?' 'Can I just order some side dishes?' 'Is there oil in this salad?' 'Can I just have some boiled chicken?' They are often more concerned with the quantity than the quality of their food, and display a unique ability to locate the nearest McDonalds.

Americans' view of Europe Bad teeth and meaningless sex. They are invariably surprised by the lack of fog in London. Some American women are inexplicably awed by posh English accents, but find anything else – regional accents, for instance – incomprehensible. Opinions such as the following are widely held: 'I thought France was very dirty and found that the French have no sense of personal space because they always seem to get right in your face. I also think all the people in France need to take their driver's test over.'

Spring Break If Brits have the Ibiza Lobster to spray foreign resorts with beer, blood and vomit, the Americans have Spring Breakers, gathering in their tens of thousands every year in resorts such as Cancun, Mexico, to indulge in sordid escapades while their parents aren't watching. Here are nine things you probably never wanted to know about Spring Break:

• The record for the most sexual partners during one Spring Break is held by Norma Jean Conacher, a native of Boston who in 1976 had sex with 413 men and 1 woman in a Daytona Beach, Florida motel. Although she is today a happily married mother of three, she plans to break the record some time in the future.

- The record for the largest number of moonies pulled in one Spring Break night was achieved on 17 March 1989, at Key West, Florida.
- The first student to drink 69 beers consecutively during a Spring Break was Billy McAllister, who performed the feat in Fort Lauderdale on 10 March 1956. It took him just four hours and ten minutes to finish the beers. He later also set the record for the longest piss, urinating for one hour and twenty minutes.
- The record for the longest-distance projectile vomiting goes to Barton Knudson of Buffalo, New York. On 23 March 1997 in West Palm Beach, Florida, after eating 32 jelly doughnuts, a garlic pizza, three hotdogs and a rack of ribs, along with a bottle of gin and a six-pack of beer, Mr Knudson vomited fifteen feet.
- During Spring Break 1996 in Panama City, Florida, Olf Kotez, a German exchange student, had three tattoos each night for a week, returning over and over again to the tattoo parlour in a drunken haze, giving him the record for the most tattoos had by a drunk man during Spring Break.
- The record for the most students arrested during one Spring Break goes to the University of Flattsburg, with 322 students thrown in the slammer in 1982 following a riot at Fort Lauderdale's Florida strip.
- The record for the most naked women spotted in one Spring Break was set on the night of 13 March 1997 in

Pompano Beach, Florida. A local bar promoted free drinks to any women showing up naked, with the result that an estimated 515 naked women were spotted wandering the streets. A record number of hard-ons was also noted.

- The most wet T-shirt contests in one night record – 498 – took place on the Spring Break night of 15 March 1979 in Fort Lauderdale. Twenty-five different bars held the contests, some holding one each and every hour until closing.

- The record number of drunk students falling to their death in one place during one Spring Break is fifteen, at Adolph's Crescent Ring Motel and Baglerama, in Boca Raton, Florida. The students took a plunge after trying to climb balconies to neighbouring rooms.

Likely to say:

'What's that in real money?'

'If this is Monday, it must be Belgium.'

'I'm Irish.'

'In America the roads are a lot bigger.'

'In America the beer is cold.'

'Wanna huck some darts?'

'What do you mean, you don't have room service?' and other general refusals to accept answers they don't like.

UK

'We don't bother much about dress and manners in England, because as a nation we don't dress well and we've no manners.'

George Bernard Shaw, *You Never Can Tell* (1898), Act One

Tales of British misbehaviour abroad are so plentiful that the tourist equivalent to leprosy has been given its own chapter at the beginning of this book. But there's always room for more, and here both classes of British tourist – the Ibiza Lobster and the Polite Peruvian Explorer – are treated with the disdain they so richly deserve.

The Ibiza Lobster

Loud and drunk Many Brits abroad treat their holiday as an extended Saturday night out. This involves drinking to excess, crap sex, fighting and puking. The fact that alcohol tends to be cheaper in package resorts than it is at home, and that nobody knows them at the resort, makes many feel they have licence to behave even more badly than they would at home. Brits abroad love pub crawls and binge drinking. They are notorious in Continental Europe for their heavy drinking, especially their consumption of spirits; related to this is the widespread reputation of British girls on holiday to be 'easy' and sexually available. Loud British drunken tomfoolery has received heavy exposure in the European media but is probably no worse than Americans on Spring Break in Cancun or Australians in Bali.

Food 'We sell chips!' And proper soggy English chips, not those fucking French fries. Favourite meals include egg and chips, chips and gravy, and full English breakfast, with imported Walls sausages. The more adventurous might try paella, or curry sauce on their chips for an 'exotic' food kick.

Baked beans, PG Tips and HP sauce are occasionally taken on holiday owing to the difficulty of sourcing such essentials abroad.

Physical attributes Sunburn. Brits abroad excel in the inappropriate exposure of flesh, especially when showing off their tacky tattoos. Some add to this by mooning or baring their breasts at any available opportunity. Several years in popular resorts tends to give skin walnut consistency and an alarming orange colour, especially in the women.

Clothes Burberry hats and handbags. Sportswear. Women: Cropped tops, thong backs clearly visible. Men: football shirts, arse cracks clearly visible.

Behaviour Brits abroad find it difficult to integrate into local communities, as they are reluctant to learn local languages – 'I've been here for three days now and if they haven't learned English yet that's their problem' – and assume that English will always be understood if spoken slowly and loudly enough. They tend to take over an area, whether as tourists or expatriates: bizarrely the Spanish complain about wanting Gibraltar back, but seem oblivious to the colonisation of parts of their Mediterranean coast by the British.

Brits abroad complain, loudly and about everything, and tend to complain more the less they have paid for their holidays. Alcohol-pickled ideas about 'Great' Britain and the British Empire, and the unquestioned inferiority of everything foreign, inform such complaints; anybody except themselves is blamed for any problems. They congregate in places with names like 'The English Pub' or anywhere with Sky Sports. They can be handy with a broken bottle, so don't look at their girlfriends.

Continental Europe is generally despised, with views such as the following commonly held: 'I went into the bogs, opened the door, and what did I find? A toilet? No! A fucking hole in the floor with a roll of bog paper on the wall. Was I supposed to shit in that? It was more like a fucking shower cubicle. Stupid French bastards.'

Brits claim to love animals, and consider other countries barbaric for not living up to their own standards of animal treatment. Such as those found in their battery chicken farms, for instance.

Personal hygiene While Brits routinely accuse the French of smelling bad (lack of soap, indulgence in garlic etc.), compare the following anecdote from a former employee of Disneyland:

The biggest problem with the Brits is the lack of hygiene. In the summer, many had very bad BO (and not just the men). They always seemed to wear tank tops and have really bad tattoos too. I can't imagine the horror of being trapped with a group of them in the elevator. After they'd get out, you could still smell them. Sometimes it was so bad we'd hold the lift and get Lysol to kill the smell. (BN, Miami)

Likely to say:

'Tits out for the lads!' (boys)

'Get yer cock out!' (girls)

'Are you called Penny? Cos I've always wanted to come into money.' (accompanied by hand thrusting up skirt/top)

'If it wasn't for the English you'd be Krauts.'

'Remember, lads, you've won the first lottery of life . . . you were born British.'

The Polite Peruvian Explorer

Divided from Ibiza Lobsters by education, social class and cultural interests, the Polite Peruvian Explorer looks with disdain on package holidaymakers frolicking in their vomit-stained Gomorrahs. But these sensitive souls have their own tourist sins to answer for. Polite Peruvian Explorers tend to eschew the developed world on holiday, realising that Daddy's money will go much further in an unspoilt – i.e. poor – country. Yet for all their protestations that they are immersing themselves in a foreign culture, their principal relationship with locals is defined either by money – as purveyors of tourist comfort and 'authenticity' – or by cameras, with which the hardy adventurers catalogue their travels, to show their friends in Islington how brave they have been when they get back home. When Polite Peruvian Explorers meet each other they tend to huddle, pretending to like football and to have worked for the money that they are travelling with. Their other characteristics include the following:

Wearing ethnic clothing Despite the fact that the characteristic clothes for men in India, for instance, are white shirts and suit trousers, many Polite Peruvian Explorers on arrival in the country dress in a bizarre mishmash of badly dyed sarongs and beaded waistcoats, which local tailors have been producing for drug-addled visitors since the 1960s. They often allow their hair to become bedraggled and matted, and are confused by locals' lack of respect for their unkempt appearance. Many protest, 'But I'm British!' upon being refused entry to prestigious establishments because of their soiled clothes; they secretly yearn for the days of the British Empire, constructed in their minds as a benevolent colonialism that was a paradise for its subjects, unlike the tyrannical regimes enforced by the Belgians or French.

Staying in ashrams Principally applicable to visitors to the Indian subcontinent, this involves public-school ditzes 'finding themselves' by eating clay in overpriced retreats. Some parents, alarmed by their children's novel sartorial choices – saffron robes and shaved heads – and anti-materialist babble on their return from an ashram, employ cult de-programmers to rewire them back on to the stockbroker path.

Some ashram leaders have come under heavy fire in the last few decades, following incidents involving the total psychic collapse of therapy-skewed acolytes and deaths resulting from poor nutrition and STDs. Nowadays most ashram leaders appear to have learned their lesson, and disciples are now recognisable only by their glazed expression and talk of 'blood purification', rather than the withered limbs and purulent genitalia that used to characterise the breed.

Calling themselves 'travellers' – rather than 'tourists'. So what's the difference? 'Travellers' tend to give less money to local communities, seek out contact with fragile cultures that will be negatively affected by their visits, and avoid places that too many other 'travellers' have visited, as they are now 'spoilt'. Ultimately, unless you work in a foreign country, you are a tourist, like it or not; and it's not at all obvious that 'travellers' have a less deleterious effect on a foreign culture than the much-maligned package tourists.

Taking too many drugs Does travel really 'broaden the mind' when it involves nothing more than sitting around in dark rooms smoking bongs or chillums all day? Probably not. While drug use in itself is not necessarily a bad thing, on the 'traveller' scene it is intimately associated with trance music, which immediately taints it with the worst possible stain.

Likely to say:
    'Pass the bong, Rupert.'
    'Feel this, it's alpaca.'
    'I've been travelling for six months now.'
    'It was just like *Fear and Loathing*.'
    'Osho says we shouldn't wear underwear as it blocks the vibrations of our feminine energy.'
    'My chakras are blocked.'

Australia

Loud and drunk Australians are occasionally even more obnoxious than the Brits, especially in resorts close to home such as Bali, speaking in endless profanities that can be heard a mile off. They are often in trouble with the police, especially near Irish or Australian pubs where they can be heard chanting 'Aussie aussie aussie, oi oi oi!' at ear-bleeding volume.

Behaviour Insane. Australians are keen to congregate around Irish or Australian pubs, where they can point out the superiority of Australia over other countries. They often bleed areas dry of alcohol before others (apart from Kiwis) can get a drink, and tend to be oblivious to their surroundings, unless access to beer or Vegemite is restricted.

Many Australian tourists have to be the centre of attention. Being so isolated, Aussies have no idea how to interact with people of other nations, and consequently expect to be the centre of attention. Tend to be extremely nationalistic, waving and distributing koalas and kangaroos to the locals. I saw one group of Australians give a kangaroo to a family in Peru, who thought it was a rat. (GH, Stockport)

Most likely to say:
   'Hey mate, you gonna fuck her, or shall I?'
   'You're as welcome here as a glass of warm beer.'
   'Here is a wattle. It's the emblem of our land. You can stick it in a bottle, or hold it in your hand.'

202

'Where's the dunny, mate? Me guts are a bit crook.'

Israel

Behaviour Rude. Many assume Israelis are only like this on holiday, but in fact they are like this at home, and are just as pushy and rude to each other as they are to other tourists and locals. Thai tourist guides are paid double when showing groups from Israel around as it's such hard work.

They almost always travel around in large groups, and eat in restaurants and stay in hotels and guesthouses that cater specifically for Israelis. Some guesthouses, by contrast, refuse entry to groups of Israelis. I stayed in a 'Casa Shalom' once and was the sole non-Israeli tenant; on asking a girl there why they always travelled in such large groups, she told me with a straight face that it was 'because everyone's trying to kill us'.

Some wear bindis as part of their subscription to the global trance party scene, and sit in their hotel rooms smoking bongs wherever they are. They are often convinced they are being ripped off, and try to pay as little as possible to local people. The following anecdote gives an example:

On the bus trip from Manali to Delhi we were about twelve Westerners, about half of them Israelis. Well, anyone who's been backpacking probably knows the reputation Israeli backpackers have, and how they indeed often behave rudely. The bus ticket cost 1,000 Indian rupees (roughly $23), and on top of that a man who secured the luggage on the bus rooftop wanted five rupees (about ten cents US). I tried, laughing, to avoid that by carrying mine and Kathrin's bags to the rooftop myself, but no – everyone had to pay. This did not please the Israelis, though, of whom one aggressively refused to pay the older man his bread money. Kathrin and another German woman tried to calm the young guy down, but he shouted at them too, telling them that he 'had lived in Bombay for two years and so knew that everyone in India wants to cheat you' (good argument for being impolite towards the locals, eh?). He sought refuge among his fellow countrymen, all of them grumpy about the extra five rupees. I feel sorry for the 'good' and 'proper' Israeli travellers; guys like these are in a big majority among the travellers from that country. Between 20 and 22 years old and straight out of three years in the army, now roaming the world wreaking havoc everywhere they go. That in no way justifies bad behaviour though, and is even a bad excuse for it . . .

When we got to the campsite halfway down, in a group the Israelis attacked the campsite owner about the high (?) prices for the tents – 100 rupees, about $2.50 per person. Well, they knocked the price down 50 cents each after having surrounded and argued with the campsite manager for fifteen minutes. I couldn't be bothered to make an effort myself, or to make myself unpopular . . .

I talked to the Israeli guy we'd tried to calm down earlier, and told him I was sick and tired of hearing Israelis arguing over peanuts. But he had a justification for everything: his view was that Israelis on average spend more money than the everyday backpacker – 'for instance Israelis always buy mineral water, but I have seen Canadians purify tap water'. That and similar arguments as to why Israelis may behave badly finally made me realise that the guy was beyond saving . . . (SM, Vienna)

Many hoteliers in the Egyptian Red Sea resorts insist on inspecting the rooms after Israeli tourists to ensure that towels, bathroom mats and lamps are present before they check them out . . . I saw this repeatedly in Taba, an Egyptian resort popular with Israeli tourists. (CA, Barcelona)

Most likely to say:
   'Give me the salt.'
   'I'm not a soldier, I'm a warrior.'
   'You mean we have to wait in line?'

Germany
Appearance The women often go topless in inappropriate places, while the men enjoy wearing thong bottoms, whatever the size of their belly and however well (or badly) the thong covers their bits. Naturism is popular, as is a lack of shame probably liberating for all but the spectator.

Behaviour According to the Italians, eating potatoes and burping in Rimini. Otherwise they are adventurous, often keen to integrate themselves into local communities and indulge in activities such as epic hiking or nude sunbathing. Or sex tourism. Wherever you go in the world there will always be at least one German, and they will usually have bagged the best place to be, by the pool, beach etc. This represents one of Bush's crucial failings in putting together a European coalition for his invasion of Iraq: the Germans could have supplied a crack troop of package tourists to take the beaches and key vantage points, leaving more troops to guard supply lines.

In a similar way to the British on the Costa del Sol, they tend to take over an area and buy up all the property. In Mallorca laws have been passed recently preventing shop-keepers from displaying information solely in German and thus encouraging richer German shoppers and discouraging their poorer Mallorcan counterparts.

They are unable to understand why their beloved black bread is not served for breakfast over the rest of the world, and are often arrogant, as in the following anecdote:

In the buses in Rio, there is an area in the back where you get on. You don't have to pay as soon as you get on; you can linger in the back area of the bus for a while before you pay the guy at the turnstile. I was on the bus when a number of very loud Germans got on – and they seemed to assume that no one could possibly understand what they were saying.

First, they said they would pretend not to understand the function of the back area of the bus and that they would not pay (nice one – abuse the public resources of an impoverished country). And then they were talking about how many black women they planned to sleep with every day, and the fake offers they would make to marry them. (SW, Preston)

Or, indeed, these:

While in Punta Arenas, Chile, having just finished an amazing trip at Torres del Paine Park, my friend and I went into a local joint for a quick dinner before collapsing into bed. We were seated next to a group of ten or so Germans. Suddenly they turned around and began to point at us and laugh uproariously. At first we thought they were just laughing at something else, but no, they were laughing at us and said, in English, 'Oh, we are Americans!' in a mocking way, for no good reason as far as I could see. My friend asked, in Spanish, if they needed anything, and they just laughed harder. We looked at the waiter who just shrugged. As an American, I have to deal with lots of comments about my compatriots (often justified, I admit), but many others and I make an effort to be respectful to both hosts and fellow tourists. (EG, Orlando)

Another incident took place in Ciudad del Este, Paraguay, in 1995. I had spent the day at Foz do Iguaçu and had just returned to my hotel's lobby. I had been hiking in the hot sun in my shorts, T-shirt and day pack, and I was hot, sweaty, and I'm sure I looked horrid.

A group of elderly German tourists were in the lobby, and one particularly obnoxious old man was pointing at me as if I was an animal at the zoo, and wanted to take a photo of me. I got closer to the guy, turned my back to him, farted as loudly as I could and left. If I could have done it again, I would have given him the Hitler salute. (EG, Orlando)

207

Japan

Behaviour The Japanese record everything with assiduous care. This stereotype has been around for a while but shows no signs of losing steam. Since the advent of cheap digital technology tourists from most nations have also attempted to record their holidays assiduously, but the Japanese are marked out by their willingness to focus on material most other tourists would disregard: reports of activities like a Japanese tourist taking a whole roll of film on a municipal rubbish bin in Heidelberg, Germany, are not unusual. They are also occasionally known for being pushy with their cameras:

A Japanese man, who was videotaping everything for sale, bumped into me. I assumed he didn't see me because he was so busy videotaping. Wrong! Within a few seconds he rammed me again, this time with greater force. It became clear he expected me to move out of the way so he could continue his videotaping with no interruptions. I turned to him and said, 'STOP THAT NOW.' I have no clue if he understood English, but he understood the look on my face. (SW, San Diego)

They also characteristically travel around in large groups, usually with tour buses, and never stray too far from air conditioning. Japanese tour groups are notorious for queue-barging, using the none-too-subtle technique described below:

So I go to the Vatican Museums one morning, shortly before they open. The line is already several blocks long. Just as I reach the end and get in line, a Japanese teenage girl runs up and crowds in front of me. No big deal; I don't say anything. The line continues to grow behind me. Then *an entire tour busload of Japanese tourists*, including the driver, arrive and join the girl in front of me. She had been sent ahead to hold a place in line. I was furious, but there seemed to be nothing I could do about it. (TM, Austin)

At the Uffizi, one Japanese woman at the head of the line tried to go back and bring ten of her peers in ahead of the fifteen or so people in the queue – there was a mild revolt which squelched that – but it wasn't for want of trying on their part. (HF, Fort Worth)

France

Behaviour The French are delighted to find other people speaking French, as they regard English as a barbaric language. They are often rude and arrogant, especially the Parisian French, who are disdainful of anyone from anywhere else, and are commonly despised themselves by the rural French:

I was in Italy, on a crowded train. A female French tourist came into the carriage and asked me to lift her bag up onto the rack. I did this, but when I turned around to sit back down, she had planted herself in my seat, shut the blind (beautiful view of the Mediterranean), and was pretending to be asleep. (AS, Mersea)

Personal hygiene They are routinely considered to smell bad, a stereotype supported by popular belief that the French use the least soap in Europe. But the mayor of ritzy resort town La Grand-Motte on the southern French coast kicked off an odour backlash in July 2002 by bringing in a law that allows police to stop people who are leaving the beach in swimwear for an odour check. When asked why he wanted to bring in such a law, the mayor said: 'I am on the terrace of one of my favourite restaurants trying to enjoy good food and wine, and then a smelly tourist comes in and ruins everything.'

The mayor maintained that Britons were among the worst offenders, and put up signs to make it clear to people what they can and cannot wear in town. As a special 'goodwill' gesture the mayor generously arranged for special T-shirts to be handed out to those who fell foul of the smell police, a move local hoteliers were appalled by. One pointed out, 'He's mad. People will of course refuse to wear them – each T-shirt is effectively saying "I smell".'

French teenagers Tend to stand around and block the pavement in an annoying fashion, and always wear their backpacks back to front.

Italy
Appearance Men: thong bikini bottoms on beach. Women: string bikinis in inappropriate locales, e.g. Muslim countries.

Italian teenagers Are known to go on shoplifting rampages when abroad, often first stealing a suitcase to take their 'souvenirs' home in. They always travel around in groups of thirty or more, allowing them to 'steam' shops and other areas with ease.

Loud Notorious for their loudness and propensity for queue-barging. Most Italian shops have given up on voluntary queue systems, and have replaced them with ticketed queues.

Faking it Italians sometimes pretend to go on holiday and then stay at home. According to a survey published in the Rome daily *Il Messaggero* in 2003, around three million Italians fake their holidays. The phenomenon has been around for a while – it even supplied the plot of a film, *Mari del Sud*, in which an executive locks himself and his family in a cellar for two weeks over the summer rather than admit he lacks the money to go on holiday. But the survey revealed the full extent of the phenomenon, suggesting that 19 per cent of Italians were not planning on taking a holiday in 2003, for reasons ranging from financial problems to poor health; and that of these, almost a third intended to pretend that they were on holiday. While most of these fantasy holidaymakers planned to buy a guidebook and read up on the resorts they'd pretended to visit, some planned to back up their story with more evidence: 24 per cent were going to buy a UV light for a fake tan, and 19 per cent were going to take their plants to a neighbour to be watered while they were away.

A psychologist interviewed by the paper commented on the

findings: 'A lot of interpersonal relationships are fake or superficial. People go to their address books and find they don't have a friend with whom to go on holiday. In the end, they stay put, as if paralysed in the presence of a huge inner emptiness.'

AFTERWORD

Travel to far-flung places has never been cheaper. The massive rise in noise and air pollution from the boom in cheap flights is considered a necessary evil, much like road fatalities; it encourages economic growth, with a whole raft of new unskilled job positions to fill for puny wages. And tourism is good business for the country visited. Don't listen to the locals in Bali who argued that the Kuta nightclub bombing had a positive effect in slowing down the devastation of mass tourism; or the reports from ecologists that jungle safaris and mountain treks are destroying these fragile environments. These rent-a-quote whiners are probably just annoyed that they aren't making any money out of the tourists, who are surely ambassadors for their country, taking nothing but photographs and leaving nothing but footprints.

Tourism enables different cultures to experience each other at first hand. British tourists in Ibiza can indulge their taste for Mediterranean hedonism by shagging and fighting other British tourists in the exotic surroundings of The English Pub and Dave's Sports Bar, while those seeking closer contact with a foreign culture can frequent the strip joints of Pattaya and Amsterdam. And if in doubt, just remember: travel broadens the mind. Doesn't it?